IMMIGRATION

Welcome or Not?

Lila Perl and Erin L. McCoy

Cavendish
Square

New York

Library of Congress Cataloging-in-Publication Data

Names: Perl, Lila, author. | McCoy, Erin L., author.
Title: Immigration : welcome or not? / Lila Perl and Erin L. McCoy.
Description: First edition. | New York, NY : Cavendish Square, 2019. |
Series: Today's debates | Audience: Grades 7-12. | Summary: "A book for
high school students about the history and controversy surrounding
immigration to the United States"-- Provided by publisher. |
Includes bibliographical references and index.
Identifiers: LCCN 2018018463 (print) | LCCN 2018028273 (ebook) |
ISBN 9781502643339 (ebook) | ISBN 9781502643322 (library bound) |
ISBN 9781502643315 (pbk.)
Subjects: LCSH: United States--Emigration and immigration--Juvenile
literature. | Immigrants--United States--Juvenile literature.
Classification: LCC JV6465 (ebook) | LCC JV6465 .P37 2019 (print) |
DDC 304.8/73--dc23
LC record available at https://lccn.loc.gov/2018018463

Editorial Director: David McNamara
Copy Editor: Rebecca Rohan
Associate Art Director: Alan Sliwinski
Designer: Ellina Litmanovich
Production Coordinator: Karol Szymczuk
Photo Research: J8 Media

CONTENTS

INTRODUCTION

Throughout the country, protesters were gathering. From New York to Nevada to Washington, DC, a group of people known as Dreamers and their supporters marched, chanted, and waved signs declaring "No Person Is Illegal" and "This Is Our Home." They chained themselves together and blocked an intersection near the US Capitol building, where at least sixty-eight people were arrested. Veronica Paute of Westchester, New York, held up a bright-orange paper flower and wore a shirt bearing a photo of her brother, Cristobal. Cristobal was one of the Dreamers, Veronica said—young people who, because they immigrated to the United States before turning sixteen years old, were temporarily allowed to remain in the country. Now, he was being detained by immigration officials.

Opposite: Thousands march in Los Angeles, California, on September 10, 2017, to protest the end of the Deferred Action for Childhood Arrivals (DACA) program.

The DACA Debate

All these rallies were taking place on March 5, 2018, the day that the Deferred Action for Childhood Arrivals (DACA) program was slated to come to an end. A US Supreme Court ruling had delayed that date for a period of up to a year, but Dreamers remained nervous. This was just the latest in a series of delays keeping the program alive. DACA was introduced in 2012 by President Barack Obama as a memorandum from the Secretary of Homeland Security. It was enacted in response to the failure of the US Congress to pass the Development, Relief, and Education for Alien Minors (DREAM) Act. "I have said time and time and time again to Congress that, send me the DREAM Act, put it on my desk, and I will sign it right away," President Obama said as he announced DACA in the White House Rose Garden on June 15, 2012. He added that to make such a policy permanent would eventually require the passage of the DREAM Act or a law like it: "It's not a permanent fix. This is a temporary stopgap measure that lets us focus our resources wisely while giving a degree of relief and hope to talented, driven, patriotic young people."

DACA was aimed at helping people who were brought to the country when they were too young to have made the choice themselves. In the past, many people had been deported to countries they didn't remember living in—and where many didn't speak the language—because they had been born there. Many immigrants' families had been torn apart because of such policies. Under DACA, Dreamers were now able to apply for a renewable Temporary Protected Status that would permit them to stay in the country legally for two years at a time. Recipients were allowed to get work permits; access in-state tuition, grants, and loans to pursue higher education; get driver's licenses in some states; and, in many cases, apply for state-subsidized health care. It did not offer a path to citizenship.

Nearly eight hundred thousand people were approved to remain in the country under DACA between 2012 and 2017. By 2018, DACA recipients were between sixteen and thirty-five years old, and had entered the United States at the median age of six. The vast majority of beneficiaries had immigrated from Mexico. More than one in four lived in California.

Mila Ipek Acar is a resident of New York City whose family moved from Turkey when she was about six years old. She says that DACA gave her the ability to build a life and a career in the United States. Her immigration status might have otherwise prevented her from doing this, since a driver's license or other proof of identification is often a basic requirement when applying for work or educational opportunities. "I was able to get a job for the first time, I was allowed to get my license, and go to college. To have hope about my future. Currently I'm studying communication and media, with no federal student aid as I did not qualify as a DACA student, just the scholarships and grants I earned in school," Acar explains. "I'm 21 years old and spent 15 of those years in the USA. This is my home and I'm here to stay."

Others argue that DACA cannot be part of the United States' long-term immigration policy. "Granting legal status to Dreamers could potentially cause a domino effect in which other families bring young children, hoping that in time their children will be granted legal status," argues Jaclyn Haak, a nineteen-year-old college student. Huy Pham, a thirty-nine-year-old Minnesota resident who immigrated from Vietnam as a toddler, argues that all immigrants should seek legal avenues of entering the country. "If we can do it the legal way, so can they," Pham told the *New York Times*. "We don't have to be creating new programs or giving them preferential treatment."

No matter whether they support the policy or not, most agree that DACA is not the legal mechanism by which such a program should continue; rather, as President Obama said in 2012, a law must be passed by the federal legislature to make such a policy permanent. The DREAM Act was first introduced in Congress in 2001. Since then, numerous iterations of the bill have been introduced, but none have passed. In late 2017 and early 2018, Democratic and Republican lawmakers alike sought and failed to pass protections for the Dreamers, as other political dealings surrounding border security and immigration policy prevented them from reaching an accord. This failure frustrated many voters, given that 73 percent of Americans supported legal protections for Dreamers in a January 2018 poll.

Immigration and Prejudice

The immigration debate has been going on in the United States—which has always been a nation of immigrants—since at least the early 1800s. Long before the days of nationhood, uninvited peoples set foot upon American shores, beginning with the earliest human migrants who trekked across the Bering Strait land bridge from Siberia to Alaska at least twelve thousand years ago.

One-fifth of the world's migrant population lived in the United States in 2017—a total of roughly 44 million people. The largest proportion of immigrants—51 percent—in the country in 2016 were from Latin America. In fact, the Migration Policy Institute reports that about 35 percent of all immigrants come from just four Central American countries: Cuba, the Dominican Republic, El Salvador, and Mexico (which has the largest number of immigrants at 11.6 million). Immigrants from Asia comprised the next-largest group at 31 percent.

Who were the first immigrants to the United States? The earliest human settlers arrived by crossing a land bridge from East Asia and became known as the Native Americans. For thousands of years, the continents of North and South America were populated by countless tribes, each with their own cultural practices, belief systems, and ways of life. Early Norse peoples are believed to have arrived at what is today the Canadian island of Newfoundland around a thousand years ago. The first Spanish settlement was established early in the sixteenth century, and more and more colonists began to arrive after that.

Some Americans today feel that the culture of the United States has been historically white and of European background, and that the arrival of new, nonwhite immigrants threatens to change the traditional culture of the country. Such groups have organized rallies in recent years where anti-Semitic (anti-Jewish), white supremacist, and racist sentiments have been expressed. However, given that the earliest humans on the continent were Native Americans and that the earliest European colonists were a diverse group, the story is in fact much more complex.

"By 1790, when the first federal census was conducted, the population of what is now the United States is estimated to have been about 64 percent white," notes Sam Roberts in his book, *Who We Are Now*. This is comparable to today's racial makeup: 61 percent of people in the United States specify that they are white and not of Hispanic or Latino origin. (Hispanic, Latino, or Spanish origin is separate from race, since a person from one of these groups can be any race, the US Census points out. Rather, these terms refer to nationality groups, heritage, lineage, or country of birth.) England, Germany, and the Netherlands accounted for most of the white population by 1790. Of the remaining inhabitants, 16 percent were Native Americans, and 11 percent were African Americans held captive against their will as a slave-labor force.

It was not until the mid-1800s that the Hispanic presence in the southwestern United States suddenly grew to about eighty thousand. This leap in numbers came with the annexation of Texas from Mexico in 1845 and with the Mexican Cession after the Mexican-American War of 1846–1848. In fact, one common misconception is that all Hispanic Americans are immigrants or

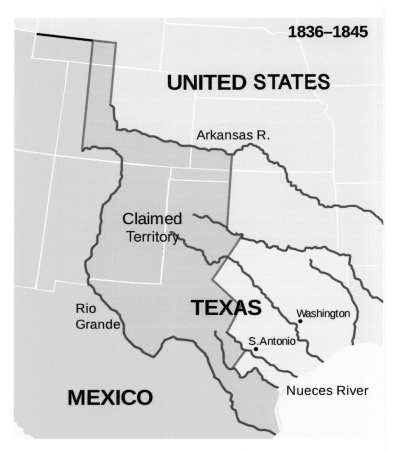

1836–1845

UNITED STATES

Arkansas R.

Claimed Territory

Rio Grande

TEXAS

Washington

S.Antonio

MEXICO

Nueces River

Texas was once a part of Mexico, after which it was an independent nation for almost ten years. Many Texans are of Hispanic origin.

the children of immigrants, when in fact, many such families have lived in the country for well over a hundred years.

In ceding the spoils of war to the United States, Mexico yielded up territory that would become the states of California, Arizona, New Mexico, Nevada, and Utah, and parts of Colorado, Kansas, and Wyoming. A new border was drawn between the two countries. Since the mid-1800s, it has stretched 2,000 miles (3,219 kilometers), partly through harsh desert terrain. Between Mexico and the state of Texas, however, the river known as the Rio Grande makes up 1,250 miles (2,012 km) of that border.

The two nations of Mexico and the United States were destined to develop very differently—politically and economically as well as culturally. Beginning in the early 1900s, Mexico was beset by a series of revolutionary upheavals led by colorful but unstable folk heroes and bandit-generals. Violence, terror, and widespread poverty throughout Mexico led to what became known as the Great Migration. Between 1910 and 1930, the Mexican population in the United States increased from 250,000 to one million.

Jobs in mining, railroading, forestry, and farming were the lure, largely the result of unmet labor needs in the United States due to both World War I and a ban on Asian immigration. No matter how rugged the living conditions or how grueling the work, many newly arrived Mexicans were willing to labor up to fourteen hours a day for minimal wages. Soon, whole families—including young children and the elderly—were working as agricultural migrants. They followed the seasons and the harvests, picking cotton and sugar beets in Texas, grapes in California, and cherries and apples in Oregon and Washington.

In time, the migrants began to settle together in neighborhoods known as barrios in the larger cities of the Southwest. Their growing numbers and more visible presence evoked prejudice on the part of whites, similar to that directed at African Americans. Mexicans could not be served in whites-only restaurants or barbershops, use white bathrooms or drinking fountains, or worship at many of the churches attended by Caucasians.

A checkered history marks the hundred-year period between the Great Migration of the early 1900s and the present. During World Wars I and II, the United States not only welcomed but recruited Hispanic immigrants to fill jobs on the home front while US citizens went to war. On the other hand, during times of economic downturn and especially during the Great Depression of the 1930s, deportations to Mexico were widespread.

Overall, the number of Americans who can trace their roots to the Hispanic nations of the Americas has grown and continues to grow. In 2016, 17.8 percent of the US population identified as Hispanic or Latino. They constitute the largest minority in the United States, exceeding African Americans, who comprise 13.3 percent of the population.

The Debate

Some Americans are alarmed because they feel that an influx of people from different cultures will change the culture of the United States. Many more, however, are disturbed because an estimated 11.1 million immigrants within the country's borders are undocumented.

Clearly, the national debate on immigration is not only a social issue—it is also economic and political. To understand why some oppose undocumented immigration while others defend those who are undocumented, we have to ask ourselves some hard questions. Why, despite hazardous border crossings, fortified in part with walls and fences and monitored by the US Border Patrol, do undocumented people keep coming? And is it true—as anti-immigration activists assert—that undocumented immigrants take jobs away from American workers, use public health and education services without contributing anything toward their cost, and constitute a criminal element in American society through identity theft and other lawbreaking activities?

The extremes are as follows: Americans who are known as nativists or restrictionists believe that an all-out effort must be made to block illegal entry and that undocumented immigrants must be actively apprehended and deported. Immigrant-rights groups, on the other hand, support the idea of offering newcomers opportunity and freedom from hardship as part of the nation's traditional regard for human rights. As a result, they advocate helping the undocumented to attain legal residency and eventually citizenship.

The US Congress has on many occasions considered bills that seek a compromise between the two extremist views toward illegal immigration, especially when it comes to those crossing the porous Mexican-US border. This has been especially true since the terrorist attacks of September 11, 2001, which destroyed the World Trade Center in New York City and sections of the Pentagon in Washington, DC. While the border-crossing terrorists thus far apprehended have generally entered the United States via Canada—and have done so legally, with visas—rather than via Mexico, many lawmakers feel that the risk of enemy infiltration from the south is considerable.

Many have also argued that those who cross US borders illegally tend to be criminals. In 2015, then–presidential candidate Donald Trump made this argument: "When Mexico sends its people, they're not sending their best ... They're sending people that have lots of problems ... They're bringing drugs. They're bringing crime. They're rapists, and some, I assume, are good people." This statement stirred up a great deal of controversy, with many arguing that it broadly mischaracterized and stereotyped a whole group of people. In fact, there is little evidence for Trump's statement. A 2016 study of two hundred metropolitan areas in the United States found that, in 70 percent of these places, the immigrant population increased between 1980 and 2016 while the crime rate either stayed the same or fell.

The debate over who should be allowed to enter the country legally and what should be done about undocumented immigrants continues. To understand the issue fully, it is necessary to study historical immigration patterns; why people immigrate; what legal and illegal avenues there are for entering the country; and the arguments for and against various approaches to immigration policy.

Chapter One

CROSSING THE US-MEXICO BORDER

During the 2016 presidential campaign, then-candidate Donald Trump's principal promise to voters was that he would build a wall along the US-Mexico border to slow down or stop illegal crossings. In early 2018, he insisted that he would not approve the DREAM Act—a provision to help young, undocumented immigrants stay in the country—until such a wall was approved and funded by Congress. "We need the wall for security. We need the wall for safety. We need the wall for stopping the flow of drugs coming in," he said. Trump and his supporters pointed to the thriving drug trade that has permeated this boundary by land, by air, and by sea.

Opposite: Migrant workers carry food and water as they begin the three- to four-day journey across the US-Mexico border.

However, the vast majority of immigrants who cross this border don't do so to smuggle drugs. Rather, they enter the United States to seek work or to join families that have already immigrated. Some are refugees seeking to escape violence or natural disaster in their home countries. Many travel back and forth across the border seasonally, traveling to wherever they can find jobs and visiting their families rarely, only when they can. Why have so many immigrants from Latin America left their countries behind and sought out work or a new life in the United States? What factors determine whether they cross legally or illegally? The answers to these questions are key to understanding the complex dynamic of immigration and emigration that has characterized the Americas for well over a hundred years.

El Norte

"We left North, toward Tijuana [Mexico], and then we found out that it wasn't so easy to come to the United States. We started inquiring. We were kids. I was 14 or 15 years old. The first time we tried they caught us."

These are the words of Fernando Martínez. When they were young, Martínez and a friend were deported because they lacked legal documents, such as a student or tourist entry visa (of which only limited numbers are issued) or a work permit (for a specific job or skill). Even so, they decided to try again.

The journey was grueling. "We thought that [Tecate, near the US border, east of Tijuana] would be a better place and that we could avoid the border patrol. It was a big mistake. We were lost in the mountains for a couple of days without food … It was in January. The nights were cold." Martínez and his friend finally managed to cross the border into California near a town called Lemon Grove and then attempted to hitch a ride to San Diego. Again, they were picked up by the US Border Patrol. "We had to go back to Mexicali [a Mexican border town] and work there for a while … We stayed there for about six months until about June and we decided to try again … I ended up in Indio, California."

The story of Fernando Martínez is just one of countless similar stories of Latin Americans who have journeyed thousands of miles, either from distant regions of Mexico or from other Central American countries through Mexico in their efforts to cross into el Norte—"the North" in Spanish. Nor does the story end with Martínez's arrival in California.

After finding a job mowing lawns, Martínez became the landscaper of a church, prospered, and bought a car. However, when the car broke down on the freeway and the police discovered that the young Mexican had neither a driver's license nor insurance, he lost his vehicle and was deported for a third time.

Managing to once more cross the border into California without documents, Martínez discovered that all his belongings had been stolen. He started a new life as a crop harvester. He might have retained his status as an undocumented alien to this day, picking fruit in California, Oregon, and Washington, were it not for a measure known as the Immigration Reform and Control Act of 1986 (IRCA), which included a program for seasonal agricultural workers known as the Special Agricultural Worker (SAW) program. The SAW provision permitted undocumented immigrants who had worked in agriculture for a given period of time and had no criminal records to apply for a status that—dependent on future good behavior—could eventually lead to citizenship.

In 1998, following many difficult years as an undocumented immigrant, Fernando Martínez became a US citizen. He was one of 2.7 million people who were able to benefit under the combined IRCA and SAW programs, often referred to as amnesty measures. Amnesty is the pardoning or forgiveness of a large group of individuals by a governmental or other authority.

In 1988, a family of undocumented immigrants waits to apply for legal residency status under the Immigration Reform and Control Act.

Today, anti-immigration activists and public figures express outrage at legislative efforts to address the undocumented immigrant problem by introducing measures that might eventually lead to legal residency and possibly a path to citizenship. Such measures, including the DREAM Act, are seen as forms of amnesty.

In 2017, Republican Senator Tom Cotton of Arizona compared the DREAM Act to IRCA. "If you pass the so-called DREAM Act, it will be the single biggest amnesty in the history of the United States, even bigger than the 1986 amnesty, which Ronald Reagan said was his biggest mistake in office," Cotton said. However, the 2017 version of the bill would make about 1.5 million people eligible for green cards, whereas IRCA did the same for nearly twice as many people.

Resisting Outsiders

The small, eastern Nebraska town of Schuyler, which was settled in the late 1800s by German and Czech immigrants, had taken on a new look in the early 2000s. Walking down Main Street, there was almost nothing to suggest the one-time storefront signs or the businesses started up by the previous residents.

The old grocery store, the liquor store, the hardware store, and the dime store were now known as La Chiquita, Dos Americas, and other Spanish-language names. This is because Schuyler had become the new home of Mexican immigrants, mainly from the town of Chichihualco in the rugged mountains of Mexico's drastically poor southern state of Guerrero. Peruvians, Salvadorans, and Guatemalans had also made the journey north through Mexico to join the migrating villagers from Chichihualco.

Many of the people who once lived in Schuyler had left. The mayor explained the exodus: "There are few good jobs here. Everyone knows they can make a better living [elsewhere]."

Many old, rural towns of the Great Plains have now become the sites of meatpacking plants that are being built close to cattle ranches. The older residents of places like Schuyler are unlikely to seek employment in meatpacking, with its assembly-line discipline and hazardous, repetitive activity.

However, poor farmers from Mexico who, back in Chichihualco, struggled to produce crops in stony mountain soil are anxious to seek this employment. In the United States, they can earn in a day what would take many months to earn back home in Mexico. They can even save up enough to send money back home to their families.

It is estimated that in 2017, remittances—or money sent back home—from Hispanic immigrants living and working in the United States totaled $75 billion. The largest percentage of this money—$28.6 billion—was dispatched to Mexico, where it comprises 2.7 percent of the country's gross domestic product (GDP)—that is, the total market value of all the services and goods that a country's economy produces. For some countries, these remittances contribute much more to the economy: in Haiti, they comprise 33.6 percent of GDP; in Honduras, 19.5 percent; and in El Salvador, 18.3 percent. In Mexico, to broaden the economic benefit to all citizens, the government has encouraged families to invest these funds in small businesses rather than using them solely for purchases of goods and services.

Meanwhile, back in Schuyler and similar rural communities far from the Mexican border, many people of European heritage who have been longtime residents of the American Midwest have experienced culture shock. They often feel overwhelmed, even invaded, by people who look and sound different from them. Some of the poorest immigrants may not speak Spanish, having recently moved from remote regions of Mexico and Central America where Native American languages are still in use.

A resistance to racially and ethnically different newcomers has characterized almost the entire history of immigration in the United States. Chinese and Japanese immigrants of the late 1800s were looked upon with animosity, as were Italians and Jews at the turn of the twentieth century. Today, Hispanic immigrants, arriving in large numbers, cause some Americans to feel threatened, not only economically but culturally.

This type of animosity has almost always been rooted in an undercurrent of racism—the mistaken belief that one race is superior to another. The conviction that people identified as racially "white" are superior to other races has led to some of the worst atrocities in history, including the Holocaust and the

Coyotes, Pollos, and "la Migra"

Although many immigrants without entry permits attempt to make the crossing into the United States on their own, Mexican border towns are rife with guides—sometimes American citizens—offering their services for a fee. Known as "coyotes" for the slyness and evasiveness of their profession, these guides propose to shepherd groups of people, often families, across the border, charging $1,500 per person or more. Costs are generally higher for those who are smuggled from Central American countries other than Mexico, as well as for people who are not from Latin America.

It can be very difficult for the client (also called a "pollo," or chicken) to determine whether the coyote (or "pollero," chicken-herder) is honest and reliable. Among the immigrants, stories abound of promises broken, of money stolen, and of abandonment in desert or mountain regions where deaths are not uncommon. Some coyotes even kidnap their clients and hold them until their families pay more money.

On the other side of the border, "la Migra" (the US immigration police) is waiting. Since the 9/11 attacks, when the US Border Patrol became part of Immigration and Customs Enforcement (ICE) in the newly formed Department of Homeland Security, the agency's technology has been beefed up. Infrared cameras with telescopic lenses mounted in armored vehicles or in helicopters, whose personnel remain in constant communication with agents on the ground, can pick out human figures on the darkest nights.

Yet the border remains porous for a great many of those who are determined and desperate. The sporadic fences—like the section of 10-foot (3-meter) welded steel that stretches for 14 miles (23 km) between Tijuana and California—can be climbed. If wading or swimming across the Rio Grande into Texas becomes too dangerous, the desert that sprawls across the Mexico-Arizona border becomes the favored place of entry.

enslavement of African Americans for hundreds of years in the United States. Residue of this long history of racism tinges the immigration debate today. For one thing, Mexico is a diverse nation, populated by people of both Native American and Spanish heritage. Of Mexico's population of 124.6 million, 62 percent are mestizos—people of both Native American and Spanish/European descent—28 percent are Native Americans, and 10 percent are criollos, meaning of Spanish descent only and therefore considered white. In the United States, some nativists and restrictionists view mestizos as setting a "bad example" of racial integration in a nation like the United States, where the proportion of whites is steadily shrinking and minorities of color are proportionately increasing. The belief that whites should not have children with other races is another tenet of racist thinking.

Mexico claims to be a nation that supports racial equality and hence offers equal opportunity to all of its citizens. However, a deeper examination of Mexican society reveals a relatively weak middle class; the very rich are greatly outnumbered by the 46 percent of people who live below the poverty line. Discrepancies in income in Mexico are based in part on regional and geographical features of the country, but just as much on skin color. Whites hold most of the country's wealth, its political power, and its highest social status—as in the United States.

Jobs Americans Won't Do?

Jeff Klein, a farmer in Stockton, California, had a difficult decision to make. His family had been farming the area for four generations, but by 2016 he could no longer make a profit on his vineyards. Over the past several years, as President Barack Obama's administration increased border security and deportations, the number of laborers entering the United States had decreased. As a result, California crop production wages

Florentino Reyes picks tomatoes in a California field. Many US farmers worry that tougher immigration legislation could make it harder to find farm workers, so that food could in fact be left rotting in the fields.

had risen by 13 percent between 2010 and 2015. This was two times faster than the overall average pay in California increased during that time. Soon, newly elected Donald Trump would increase the number of immigration raids throughout the country and reiterate his promise to build a wall along the US-Mexico border. The Trump administration would argue that reducing the number of undocumented immigrants would free up more jobs for American citizens to work.

Klein could no longer afford the labor necessary to harvest his grapes. The undocumented labor force has generally been willing to accept lower wages than people authorized to work in the United States, but with the shortage of workers, they could now negotiate higher wages for themselves. "There's not enough guys, and everybody is fighting for everybody else's guys," Klein said. The Trump administration's plan to increase deportations is "killing our labor force," he added. So in October 2016, Klein decided to uproot 113,000 Chardonnay grapevines on his land. He hoped to replace them with more profitable crops in the coming years.

Another Stockton farmer responded to increased labor costs by redesigning his vineyards so they could be harvested by machine. Brad Goehring said that he couldn't retain American-born workers, even when they were being paid $20 an hour. "We've never had one come back after lunch," he said. While increasing wages might attract more people legally authorized to work, that's not the most cost-efficient approach, economist and agriculture expert Philip Martin explained to the *Los Angeles Times*. "Well before we got to $25 [an hour], there would be machines out in the fields, doing pruning or harvesting, or we would lose crops," Martin said.

The lower wages are not the only reason that many Americans are hesitant to do the agricultural work that migrant workers from Latin America travel to the United States to do. Such farming is generally seasonal work, meaning that for a large part of the year, it doesn't employ or pay nearly as many people. What's more, during high season, people often work sixty-hour weeks for months on end in grueling conditions—bending over vegetable crops for hours or climbing ladders in excessive heat or cold. Most Americans choose to seek steadier, easier work.

However, many insist that reducing the number of undocumented workers will, indeed, create more jobs for

Americans. Writing for the conservative magazine *National Review*, Mark Krikorian, executive director of the restrictionist Center for Immigration Studies, challenges the assumption that there are jobs Americans won't do. Using undocumented immigrants, guest workers, or other foreign laborers in construction, agriculture, and other economic enterprises is just an excuse to keep the door open to immigrants, Krikorian asserts.

Do we really need foreign labor in the construction trades? No, Krikorian says. Homes can be built in factories, as prefabricated units. Rather than being constructed from the ground up, requiring numerous laborers to pour cement and to lay bricks one by one, homes can be assembled onsite with the use of advanced technology. Growing and harvesting fruits and vegetables can also be done with far fewer agricultural workers, according to Krikorian. With innovative thinking and better mechanization, even highly labor-intensive produce, such as raisins, grapes, and broccoli, can be sent to market with much less labor input. The result would be fewer jobs overall, but better ones at higher wages that Americans would be willing to fill. Whether an overall reduction in the number of jobs would be balanced out by more work and improved wages for American workers is hard to determine.

Wages and Jobs

Another argument against immigration is that it drives wages down for American workers. George J. Borjas, an economics and social policy professor at the Harvard Kennedy School, explains this dynamic in a 2016 article for *POLITICO*:

> *Both low- and high-skilled natives are affected by the influx of immigrants. But because a disproportionate percentage of immigrants have few skills, it is low-skilled*

American workers … who have suffered most from this wage dip. The monetary loss is sizable. The typical high school dropout earns about $25,000 annually. According to census data, immigrants admitted in the past two decades lacking a high school diploma have increased the size of the low-skilled workforce by roughly 25 percent. As a result, the earnings of this particularly vulnerable group dropped by between $800 and $1,500 each year.

This isn't the full picture, however. "Somebody's lower wage is always somebody else's higher profit," Borjas writes. In the case of immigration, wealth is taken out of the employee's pocket and reallocated to the employer, who saves money by paying lower wages. Employers' profits increase and, in the end, the total wealth of the American-born population actually grows; by Borjas's estimation, it amounts to a $50 billion annual surplus. It's just that now, the money is in different people's possession.

When it comes to protecting American jobs, undocumented immigration is not the only factor up for debate. President Trump has sought to decrease the number of legal immigrants by roughly half, part of his goal being to leave more high-skilled jobs available for Americans. Legal immigrants "are more highly skilled than ever before," confirms William Frey, a senior fellow at research group the Brookings Institution.

However, as Borjas argues, "High-skilled immigration really can make America wealthier. The steady influx of legal immigrants also produces more taxpayers, who can assist financially as the native population ages." Dany Bahar, another senior fellow at Brookings, argues that "by cutting on immigration, the country will miss an opportunity for new inventions and ventures that could generate the jobs that the president is so committed to bring back. Thus, if the current administration wants to create jobs and

The STEM OPT (Science, Technology, Engineering, and Math Optional Practical Training) program has let thousands of international students stay in the US after graduating.

'make America great again' [the slogan of Trump's presidential campaign], it should consider enlisting more migrants." As proof of immigrants' role in growing the economy, Bahar points out that while only about 15 percent of the labor force in the United States is made up of immigrants, roughly 25 percent of entrepreneurs and investors are immigrants.

In October 2017, US Citizenship and Immigration Services ordered its staff not to automatically renew H-1B and other visas for high-skilled workers, but to more carefully scrutinize requests for renewal—an approach that would create more uncertainty and paperwork for employers, some argued. In fact, the climate around immigration had been uncertain for months, at least since January 27, 2017, when President Trump signed an executive order to prohibit immigration from seven Muslim-majority countries for a ninety-day period. The ban, believed by some to unconstitutionally target people based on their religion, was challenged in courts for months, and businesses and individuals were unsure whether it would come into effect. A February 2017 article in Seattle-based publication *GeekWire* said that, in this unstable climate, tech giants such as Microsoft and Amazon that employ thousands of people on H-1B visas might choose to shift those jobs to Canada, in which case the United States would lose sales and income tax revenue.

The Trump administration was also expected to roll back the STEM OPT (Science, Technology, Engineering, and Math Optional Practical Training) program, under which about forty-five thousand foreign students stay in the country to work after graduating. However, as Stuart Anderson argues in the magazine *Reason*, international students comprise 81 percent of electrical engineering graduate students and 79 percent of computer science students. If students don't have the opportunity to work in the United States after graduation, they will be less likely to attend American schools, Anderson insists. "Without international students, therefore, there simply wouldn't be enough students to sustain a full range of graduate level STEM course offerings, which would shrink the choices for U.S. college students," he writes.

Sweatshop Conditions

Many advocates for increasing legal immigration to the United States argue that people will continue to travel to the United States to work whether it is illegal or not, and given this fact, it is the country's responsibility to protect these workers from the sweatshop conditions in which many of them labor. The term "sweatshop" has commonly been applied to the cramped, dark, and unsanitary manufacturing establishments that sprang up in New York and other East Coast cities during the waves of immigration of the early 1900s. During those years, Italian, Jewish, and other southern and eastern European men and women labored entire lifetimes in the garment or sewing trades.

At the time, no laws existed regarding a minimum wage, maximum hours, or safe and sanitary working conditions. Rats, mice, and roaches inhabited the sweatshops. Workers died of respiratory diseases caused by fabric dust, and from horrible accidents, including fires that swept through the factories. Few sweatshops had bathrooms or drinking water, and workers weren't allowed to take breaks. Many clothing operators were paid based on how many garments they produced in a day, so they often took work home to complete at night.

Today, much of the labor-intensive garment industry that once flourished in the United States has moved abroad to China and other countries where salaries and the cost of living are lower. So it isn't surprising that the remains of that industry exist mainly in parts of the United States that have high concentrations of immigrants, many undocumented, who will work for less money and under poorer working conditions because they have no legal avenues by which to complain.

Los Angeles has long been a center of US clothing manufacturing, with many establishments employing Latin American immigrants who receive as little as three dollars an hour, well below minimum wage, and no overtime for ten- to twelve-hour days. New York, which has an ever-increasing number of Mexican immigrants, has also become the site of small underground garment factories. However underpaid they may be, these workers tend to bring valuable skills to the table, skills that may not be easily replaceable should the establishments seek to hire only American-born workers. In fact, an April 2017 survey of one hundred people in the US fashion community found that 82 percent said they hired immigrant workers because of their talent and skills—not because they would work for lower wages.

Many argue that these workers keep American manufacturing competitive in a global market. However, Krikorian blames the overuse of foreign labor on a lack of innovative thinking. Without the immigrant workforce, he argues, the manufacture of apparel would see technological advancement and greater productivity. As matters stand, the abundance of low-skilled labor leads only to stagnation.

Given so many obstacles, why do undocumented immigrants brave the difficult trek over the US-Mexico border year after year, only to work for lower pay than Americans in sometimes-grueling conditions? Is it true—as anti-immigrant activists assert—that they are making their way to the United States chiefly to collect welfare payments, obtain free education and health care, engage in criminal activities, and threaten the financial well-being of Americans? Undocumented immigrants, advocates argue, come seeking a better life for their families, and send much of the money they earn to families back home who would otherwise be living in severe poverty. Advocates also point out that, even when immigrants lack the legal documentation to work, they still contribute to the US economy by paying sales taxes on the purchases they make, by paying rent, and by having state and federal income taxes withheld from their salaries. Yet because so many use counterfeit documents to find employment, it is unlikely they will ever collect the Social Security or other benefits to which they have contributed a portion of their wages.

Learning why immigrants have chosen the United States over the course of its history may provide a more nuanced understanding of why immigration happens, and how it can impact a country's economy, people, and culture.

Chapter Two

CLOSING THE GOLDEN DOOR

As new groups of people have chosen to immigrate to the United States, they have faced varying degrees of resistance to their arrival. This resistance on the part of previous settlers, and even other immigrants, has been motivated by economic concerns, a fear of the unknown, mistaken beliefs about racial or cultural difference, political interests—or a combination of these and other factors. This is why it is so important to understand the context in which such migrations take place before evaluating the choices people made. One of the earliest moments of mass immigration to the United States came when the California Gold Rush hit.

Seeking Fortune

On January 24, 1848, the first nuggets of gold were observed in the sparkling waters of Sutter's Creek

Opposite: Around the year 1855, Chinese workers in California pan for gold during the California Gold Rush.

in California. Over the next few years, more than three hundred thousand people would travel to California to make their fortunes, and not all of them were American citizens.

In the 1850s, emigrants from China began arriving in San Francisco. The earliest of the newcomers were merchants from the Celestial Empire, as China was then known. Rather than digging for gold directly, however, the merchants made their money by supplying the miners in the gold fields with pickaxes and other tools, as well as tents, clothing, and food. They numbered only a few hundred, but because they were the first on the scene, their businesses quickly flourished. The journey across the Pacific Ocean was direct, if lengthy, compared with the much longer voyages that East Coast vessels en route to California had to make, traveling around South America's Cape Horn.

At first, the Chinese merchants in San Francisco were relatively well received. However, they were soon followed by growing numbers of Chinese peasants and laborers, most of them starving farmers and fishermen from the villages of Southeast China. Word had reached them of *gam saan*, the "golden mountain," across the sea. Some stayed only a short while, long enough to amass a few hundred dollars and return to their families with their riches. Others remained indefinitely, trying their luck in the gold fields until the precious metal began to run out in the 1860s. Then, hungry for work, many Chinese immigrants began to mine silver, quartz, and other minerals. Others became laborers, cooks, and household servants, or went on to build the roadbed for the eastbound Central Pacific Railroad through treacherous mountain terrain.

Some 2,500 Chinese laborers in California in 1851 had increased to 20,000 by 1852. The census of 1870 reported that there were 63,199 Chinese nationals in the United States, of whom at least 45,000 lived in California. By this time, the eastbound Central Pacific and the westbound Union Pacific Railroads had met at Promontory Point, Utah. On May 7, 1869, the day the two legs of the system were joined, 10,000 Chinese immigrants who had been railroad builders lost their jobs. The labor market was then flooded with people of Chinese descent who had already proved themselves willing to do the most hazardous jobs and to work for less than most Caucasians in the western states.

Racist stereotypes sprang up around these immigrants as Americans began to feel that their own jobs were threatened. The Chinese workers—the vast majority of them men—had been labeled the "yellow peril." Nativist thinkers, including political figures, saw them as an Asian army of sorts that was threatening to change the cultural makeup of the United States as it was at the time. If Chinese immigration were allowed to continue, the number of women would increase and families would expand. Their children would automatically be eligible for American citizenship.

The self-termed prophet of San Francisco, Henry George, who vehemently opposed Chinese immigration, wrote in the *New York Tribune* on May 1, 1869, "The 60,000 or 100,000 Mongolians on our Western coast are the thin edge of the wedge which has for its base the 500,000,000 of Eastern Asia … The Chinaman can live where stronger than he would starve. Give him fair play and his quality enables him to drive out stronger races."

The years between 1869 and 1882 saw a steady increase in local ordinances that were hostile to the Chinese. In San Francisco, the Sidewalk Ordinance of 1870 forbade Chinese individuals who carried shoulder poles (in lieu of having beasts of burden) from using the city sidewalks. The Queue Ordinance of 1873 led to attacks by street ruffians, who chopped off the long braids, called queues, that Chinese men wore out of respect for the Qing dynasty back home.

The Rock Springs Massacre

Following the completion of their work on the Central Pacific Railroad in 1869, many Chinese laborers fanned out along the Western Seaboard of the United States; others moved inland. As soon as they settled into their new communities, they constructed what were commonly called Chinatowns—dwelling areas that were

At least twenty-eight Chinese miners were killed in a horrific massacre that racially targeted Chinese workers in Rock Springs, Wyoming, in 1855. Others were severely wounded and would die soon after.

often looked upon with disdain by whites. Among the streets lined with living quarters and shops were rumored to be gambling houses and opium dens.

Rock Springs, a coal-mining town in the Wyoming Territory, was the site of a mine owned by the Union Pacific Railroad, which, like the Central Pacific, had employed many Chinese laborers. On September 2, 1885, the company sent a crew of four hundred Chinese workers down into one of the chambers of the mine, where they outnumbered the white crew. Infuriated that they were being hired for lower wages over white miners, one of the workers, a Welsh immigrant, attacked a Chinese man with a shovel, killing him.

After work ended, white miners assembled with rifles, then approached the Rock Springs Chinatown. They began firing at the Chinese and set fire to the immigrants' living quarters. At least twenty-eight Chinese miners died. Others who had been wounded or mutilated died soon after.

The Rock Springs Massacre, unfortunately, was not the only example of fierce anti-Chinese persecution. Because the Chinese Exclusion Act of 1882 had not ordered the deportation of those people already living in the country, many whites believed it necessary to run the immigrants out of town themselves. In 1886, the anti-Chinese citizenry of Tacoma, Washington, set the local Chinatown ablaze, forced Chinese residents into boxcars at gunpoint, and shipped them off to Portland, Oregon.

Acts of violence increased, and signs at torchlight parades announced that "The Chinese Must Go!" This motto belonged to the California Workingmen's Party, which was founded in 1877 by Dennis Kearney, an Irish immigrant who was determined to halt Chinese immigration. Then, in 1882, for the first time in its history, the US Congress passed a law prohibiting workers from a single country from landing on its shores. The federal statute was known as the Chinese Exclusion Act.

The specific purpose of the act was to ban the entry of Chinese laborers, whether skilled or unskilled. Not included in the ban were persons who might be of value politically, economically, or educationally, such as Chinese officials, merchants, tourists, teachers, and students.

Under the terms of the Chinese Exclusion Act of 1882, Chinese workers were prohibited from entering the country for a period of ten years. The act allowed those who were already in the country to remain, but with no possibility of becoming naturalized citizens. Those who wished to return to China could do so. The passage of the Geary Act ten years later, in 1892, extended the ban and required the Chinese living in the country to get a US certificate of residence—a form of identity card—or be deported.

In spite of the new restrictions, anti-Chinese violence on the West Coast continued to grow. It manifested itself in the burning of Chinese property and the mutilation and killing of Chinese people. One of the worst of these anti-immigrant uprisings was the unprovoked attack known as the Rock Springs Massacre, which took place in the territory of Wyoming in 1885. In spite of petitions for fair treatment and lawsuits seeking reparations for damages and deaths, as well as the same rights other American residents received, the Chinese continued to face severe challenges and dangerous racism.

With the passage of time, many began to drift eastward to Chicago, Boston, and New York. Rather than risk challenging whites by competing in the labor market, they focused on the ownership of small family businesses in the Chinatown communities of the larger cities. Not until 1943, when China became an ally of the United States in World War II, was the 1882 ban on Chinese immigration lifted. The Chinese Exclusion Act had remained in effect for sixty-one years.

No Irish Need Apply

Race, nationality, language, culture, and customs were among the factors that made many of the immigrants of the 1800s "too different" for most Americans to accept. Religion was another major barrier.

Many of the earliest colonists in North America were English and Protestant—but not all. Dutch Protestants had inhabited New York in its earliest days, and German Protestants were to be found in Pennsylvania. True, there were Roman Catholics in Maryland (where Protestants outnumbered them), and there were Jews in cities of the Eastern Seaboard ranging from Newport, New York City, and Philadelphia to Charleston and Savannah. However, these were minority religions in North America in the 1600s and 1700s.

Nor were fellow Protestants always on the best of terms. Benjamin Franklin, the much-admired statesman and scientist, viewed the Germans who were immigrating to Pennsylvania in the 1700s with alarm. "Why," he wrote, "should the Palatine [feudal German] Boors be suffered to swarm into our Settlements, and by herding together, establish their Language and Manners, to the Exclusion of ours? Why should Pennsylvania, founded by the English, become a Colony of Aliens, who will shortly be so numerous as to Germanize us instead of our Anglifying them?"

Another major immigrant group of the colonial period were the Scotch-Irish (not to be confused with the Irish fleeing the potato famine of the late 1840s). Like the Germans, they had left their homes for economic, political, and religious reasons. For instance, although the Scotch-Irish were Protestants, they were still not treated as equals by the Church of England unless they had been married within the precincts of the Church. Also, English law prohibited them from the foreign trade of their woolens and linens. The onset of crop failures in the early 1700s drove many Scotch-Irish to the American colonies, most as indentured servants. Once they had worked off their debts to their sponsors and employers, they tended to settle in the frontiers of the colonies of the mid-South.

By the time the American Revolution ended in 1783, the former colonies had taken on the aspect of nationhood. The German, Dutch, Scotch-Irish, and other white minorities had blended to varying degrees with the dominant English Protestant culture. The rest of the population—Native Americans and African Americans—would remain minorities, the one embattled and the other enslaved.

The 1800s heralded an age of industrial development, population growth, and migrations on a global scale. Until the 1840s, older immigration patterns of the colonial era more or less continued. However, the second half of the decade brought the first Chinese immigrants to California, as well as the Mexicans who had found themselves north of the border as a result of their country's defeat in the Mexican-American War of 1846–1848.

At about the same time as nonwhite, non-Protestant Chinese immigrants were beginning to populate the American West, the Eastern Seaboard witnessed an influx of people from Ireland. For decades, poor Irish farmers had depended on the potato crop as their staple food and as a source of income. In 1845, however, a mold began to appear on the leaves of the potato plants, and by the following year, the crop had turned to a foul-smelling rot. It was the start of the Irish Potato Famine.

Hundreds of thousands of Irish people starved to death before the famine subsided in the 1850s. In the meantime, those who could began to flee. Many went to England but many more to the United States, for a total of about one million immigrants who were overwhelmingly Roman Catholic. Potato crop failures struck again in 1863 and in the 1880s, swelling the number of Irish Catholic immigrants to four million.

An illustration from an 1850 London publication shows Irish emigrants sailing to the United States to escape the Irish Potato Famine.

The new arrivals settled mainly in the coastal cities of Boston and New York. They huddled in tenements with no running water or sanitation, slept on mounds of dirty straw, sought jobs as dock workers, and performed other kinds of manual labor. Poverty and disease among the newcomers of the 1800s put a strain on the poorhouses and hospitals of the nation. At New York's Bellevue Hospital in the 1850s, 85 percent of the foreign-born patients were Irish.

The conditions under which the unskilled Irish immigrants lived were said to be as bad as, or worse than, those of the country's African American slaves. The inevitable lack of hygiene in the immigrants' homes made them undesirable to would-be employers, who often posted signs stating "No Irish Need Apply."

Another factor fueling anti-Irish sentiment was their religion. Protestants were a majority in the United States, and many were deeply concerned that admitting Catholic immigrants in large numbers might lead to a takeover of the nation by the pope (the head of the Catholic Church) in Rome. Samuel F. B. Morse, inventor of the telegraph, warned Americans of such a possibility. His rallying cry to "shut your gates" against immigrants who worshipped in the Roman Catholic Church was echoed by the Know-Nothing Party.

The Know-Nothing movement began as a nativist response to Catholic immigration in the cities of the Eastern Seaboard. In 1845, it became a national political party and, at the same time, a secret organization. When asked about their political identity, its members would only reply that they knew nothing.

Their goal was to elect only nativist, Protestant candidates to public office and to change the naturalization process. The Know-Nothings sought to establish a residency requirement of twenty-five rather than five years for immigrants who wanted to become citizens.

Early restrictionists didn't succeed in passing laws that would require visas, literacy tests, or other barriers to citizenship. However, the hostility toward religious and ethnic groups that threatened to change the composition of the United States as it had been during the 1700s had its effect on the newcomers: they dug in their heels. The Irish clung to their Roman Catholic beliefs. Catholic French Canadians refused to give up either their religion or their language. German Lutherans conducted their Protestant church services in German.

Practically all the groups that continued to arrive throughout the nineteenth century sought the security and the camaraderie of people with whom they shared a language or cultural identity. They lived in their own neighborhoods with their own schools, churches, newspapers, and languages. They honored their own festivals, customs, and manners until succeeding generations were more ready and able to integrate.

Whether foreign-born laborers and settlers were welcomed or not, there was no question that, in the 1800s, the United States needed them to build a rapidly expanding nation—to construct its canals and railroads, to dig its mines, and to make its untilled lands productive.

The "New" Immigrants of the 1900s

Greatest in number among the southern European immigrants of the early 1900s were the Italians. A mere 32,159 had arrived in 1882. However, in 1907, the peak year for twentieth-century immigration to the United States, their number had risen nearly tenfold to 285,731.

This change in the countries of origin of many newcomers to American shores reflected the changes that had taken place in the economies of their respective nations. Those in northern and western Europe had already been emptied of their most desperate and impoverished people, and living standards for the remainder had improved.

Now, as Leonard Dinnerstein and David M. Reimers write in *Ethnic Americans*, Italians were fleeing terrible poverty back home:

> *The southern Italians, especially, fled horrendous conditions. Unemployment, high birth rates, overpopulation, cholera and malaria epidemics were only some of the problems besetting these people.*
>
> *Many of the Italian peasants lived in houses of straw or even in rock caves and abandoned Greek tombs … An agricultural laborer earned from 8 to 32 cents a day in Sicily … The resulting increase in poverty was so great that some Italian arrivals in the United States declared afterward, "We would have eaten each other if we had stayed."*

Between 1890 and 1910, the Italian population of the United States increased by three million people. The second-largest influx of the late 1800s and early 1900s consisted of Jews from eastern Europe, mainly Russia. They numbered two million.

Czarist restrictions in Russia forbade Jews from owning land and limited their occupational and educational opportunities. The poverty that resulted was one reason many Russian Jews chose to emigrate. Equally important, Jewish boys could be drafted into the Russian army at as young as twelve years old and made to serve for thirty-one years. What's more, for decades after the assassination of Czar Alexander II in 1881, government-condoned massacres known as pogroms ravaged Jewish settlements, bringing mob violence that took the form of beatings, murders, looting, and rape.

Also prominent among the new immigrants to the United states were Slavic peoples from eastern Europe, especially Poles, who numbered more than one million during the early 1900s. Most southern and eastern Europeans—Italians, Jews, Poles, Serbs, Croatians, Hungarians, and Greeks among them—settled

Prescott F. Hall was a founder of the Immigration Restriction League, which opposed the ingress of some immigrants based on their race.

in northeastern US cities, which offered a wide variety of factory and construction jobs. There, many first-generation ethnic groups carved out their own dwelling areas, neighborhoods that served as cultural niches fashioned in the image of the Old World.

Among Americans of an earlier generation, however, the new immigrants were looked upon with contempt. Italians were referred to as the "Chinese of Europe." Poles weeding onions in New England were called "Animals … with stolid, stupid faces." American novelist Henry James, in his 1907 book *The American Scene*, characterized the new immigrant as follows: "He resembles for the time the dog who sniffs around the freshly acquired bone, giving it a push and a lick."

Nor was the East Coast of the United States the only place where immigrants felt unwelcome. A number of the new immigrants of the late 1800s and the early 1900s drifted toward the Midwest and the South, where similar slurs awaited them.

A summing-up of nativist sentiment toward newcomers can be found in the words of Prescott F. Hall, a founder in 1894 of the outspoken Immigration Restriction League. According to Hall, it was imperative that Americans decide whether they wanted their country "to be peopled by British, German, and Scandinavian stock, historically free, energetic, progressive, or by Slav, Latin, and Asiatic races ["Asiatic" referred in this case to Jews] historically down-trodden, atavistic, and stagnant." These generalizations were not based in fact but in unfounded stereotypes common at the time.

At the same time that the immigrants who had recently arrived on the East Coast were experiencing prejudice, the states of the far west, especially California, were experiencing the influx of yet another Asian people—the Japanese.

The admission of Chinese laborers to the United States had, of course, been cut off by the passage of the Chinese Exclusion Act of 1882. However, the act did not extend to other potential immigrants from the Far East, such as the impoverished Japanese farmers who had begun to leave their homeland during the latter half of the 1800s to work in the sugarcane fields of the Kingdom of Hawaii.

By the 1890s, lured by the higher wages being paid in the United States, Japanese workers began arriving on the West Coast from Hawaii. At first, many worked in railroad-building, mining, and construction. However, their background was mainly in farming, and they soon brought over their wives and families and turned to growing produce for both local and distant markets. Even when a California law, passed in 1913, decreed that aliens who were ineligible for citizenship through naturalization could not buy land, many Japanese immigrants managed to acquire it through third parties—and to prosper.

Like the Chinese, the Japanese faced racism in the United States, and were quickly identified as the "yellow peril." However, they came to be feared and disliked even more than the Chinese. The US Industrial Commission declared in 1901 that the Japanese "have most of the vices of the Chinese, with none of the virtues. They underbid the Chinese in everything, and are as a class tricky, unreliable, and dishonest."

Fear of these newcomers was also engendered by the fact that, whereas China's economy at that time was relatively undeveloped, Japan was fast becoming a military and industrial power. An Alabama congressman, Richmond Pearson Hobson, stated in 1900 that the Japanese were "rushing forward with feverish haste stupendous preparations for war ... The war is to be with America."

Clearly, in the view of US nativists, the time was more than right for the enactment of an immigration law that would do something to restrict the admission of more and more arrivals from abroad. Many West Coast citizens would adopt anti-Japanese sentiments and support the passage of a law banning immigration from Asia. The Golden Door had stood wide open to many of the world's immigrants for a hundred years. Now it was swinging shut.

Chapter Three

DISCRIMINATION, GUEST WORKERS, AND REFUGEES

The outbreak of the Great War (later known as World War I) in Europe in 1914 spurred the enactment of the first US federal law placing a restriction on all immigrants, not only on the Chinese or those likely to become public charges. Discriminatory practices targeting specific groups of people were built into the immigration legislation of the next few decades. Meanwhile, the demographics of those seeking entry into the United States shifted as various events on the world stage created refugees and pushed immigrants to leave their countries to seek work and opportunity.

The Immigration Acts of 1917 and 1924

In 1917—the year the United States entered World War I—the government yielded to nativist urgings

Opposite: A mother and daughter, both immigrants to the United States, are pictured circa 1902 on Ellis Island, New York, where many immigrants to the country were processed for entry.

that the "hordes of Europe" be restrained by mandating that people pass a literacy test before they could enter the country. Some nativists demanded that immigrants prove they could read in English in order to pass the test. However, this stipulation was so unrealistic that Congress refused to consider it. Anti-immigrant feeling in America was nonetheless so strong that the literacy law passed easily, and Congress overrode the veto of President Woodrow Wilson.

As a result, all incoming immigrants older than sixteen were required to be able to read in at least one recognizable language. Another major feature of the Immigration Act of 1917 was a ban on virtually all laborers from Asia, including Japan. This was accomplished by creating a so-called Asiatic Barred Zone. The new law also increased the head tax on new arrivals to eight dollars.

These changes, though, had little effect on the inflow of immigrants. Even with literacy tests, an increased entry fee, and the examination of newcomers at the major port of entry on New York's Ellis Island, only a small fraction of arrivals faced exclusion or deportation.

Ellis Island, the immigrant processing station in Upper New York Bay, had opened in 1892, replacing the smaller onshore facility in lower Manhattan known as Castle Garden. During the peak years of ship travel, Ellis Island processed more than a million disembarking immigrants annually.

In its vast hall, doctors examined men, women, and children for communicable diseases and for chronic health or mental health problems that might result in their becoming public charges—that is, reliant on government aid for basic needs such as food and shelter. Those who could not meet the entrance requirements had their clothing marked in chalk with an identifying letter. An E stood for eye disease, an H for a heart problem, an X for a mental problem. The process of examination and interrogation was so dreaded by the new arrivals that Ellis Island became known as the Isle of Tears.

Immigration slowed during World War I and for a brief time in 1919, after the war ended. However, nativists feared a resurgence of immigration, particularly as a result of the Bolshevik Revolution in Russia. The czar had been deposed and a Communist government had taken power, threatening to spur antirevolutionary dissidents to flee the country.

The fear of another influx of immigrants along with long-established nativist leanings pushed Congress to pass the most restrictive immigration legislation to date. The Immigration Law of 1924 was also known as the Johnson-Reed Act (after its authors) and the National Origins Act. In addition to requiring for the first time both visas and photos from all immigrants, it set European quota limits based on countries of origin. These quotas strongly favored northern and western Europeans over those from the south and east. Newcomers from countries of the Western Hemisphere such as Canada and Mexico were exempt from the national quotas, as they appeared to pose no threat to nativists at the time. Another important provision of the 1924 law was the closing of the Golden Door—a nickname for Ellis Island and sometimes used to refer to US immigration in general—to Asians from a wide range of Pacific nations from Japan to Malaysia, with no exceptions. As a result, the new law was also known as the Asian Exclusion Act.

During its forty-year peak immigration period from 1880 to 1920, the United States had received 23.5 million new arrivals. In the words of Albert Johnson, the restrictionist Washington State congressman who cosponsored the 1924 act, the American people had suffered "the encroachments of the foreign-born flood upon their own lives." Johnson continued in the same vein: "The United States is our land ... We intend to maintain it so. The day of indiscriminate acceptance of all races is discredited."

The United States had created federal bureaus in 1864 and 1890 to oversee the enforcement of earlier laws. To implement the newer laws, the Immigration and Naturalization Service (INS) was established in 1933. It was originally part of the Department of Labor. In 1940, it would be transferred to the Department of Justice, and in 2003, the renamed Immigration and Customs Enforcement (ICE) would become part of the Department of Homeland Security.

In 1924, INS set up the US Border Patrol to apprehend foreigners who were trying to enter the country via the Mexican or Canadian borders. Immigrants of Mexican nationality, however, were not the main target. In spite of the growing numbers that crossed the border following the Mexican Revolution of 1910, the 450-strong organization was mainly seeking to apprehend Asians and Europeans seeking to skirt the new literacy and quota laws.

The new laws accomplished their purpose. Compared with the peak year of 1907 (1,285,349 new arrivals), immigration overall decreased to a total of four million between 1921 and 1930. During the 1930s—the major years of the Great Depression in the United States—it slowed to a mere half-million over a ten-year period.

This combination of economic hard times and tough admission laws discouraged would-be newcomers from Europe as well as elsewhere. In the early 1930s, more than four hundred thousand Mexican laborers returned home, many of them against their will and after having worked for decades in the United States. Even permanent residents and American citizens were deported. An estimated 60 percent were children born in the United States.

World War II and the Bracero Program

Meanwhile, Europe of the 1930s was being divided into opposing political camps. Italy, led by the militaristic fascist

In May 1943, at the height of World War II, agricultural workers from Mexico arrive in Stockton, California, as part of the bracero program.

dictator Benito Mussolini, and Nazi Germany, rearmed and under the command of Adolf Hitler, were forming an alliance against Great Britain, France, the Low Countries, Central Europe, and Russia.

When war broke out in Europe in September 1939, the politically isolationist United States found itself ill-prepared to offer assistance in the form of arms and food supplies to its British and French allies. Following the stock market crash of 1929, the Great Depression had wreaked economic havoc throughout the country: industry had reached a standstill and unemployment was at record highs. Large numbers of Americans waited in breadlines for food and lived in shantytowns.

On December 7, 1941, Japan attacked a US Navy base in Pearl Harbor, Hawaii. Japan was an ally of Germany and Italy in

The Sleepy Lagoon Case and the Zoot Suit Riots

In the 1940s, many Mexicans and Mexican Americans faced restrictions that prevented them from entering movie theaters, restaurants, bars, and some churches patronized by Caucasians. The teenage youth of these families often felt torn: they identified with both Mexican and

Two young men are pictured after having been stripped and beaten during the June 1943 Zoot Suit Riots.

American culture. Many dressed like other American teens by wearing zoot suits, a form of dress popular in the 1940s. This outfit for young men consisted of high-waisted trousers; a broad-shouldered, oversized jacket; a long watch chain; and a fedora hat with a flat top and broad brim.

When, on the morning of August 2, 1942, a dying young Mexican was found at a gang gathering spot known as the Sleepy Lagoon, the twenty-two members of the so-called 38th Street Club were arrested and, still in their disheveled zoot suits, charged with conspiracy to murder. Unable to pay their bail, the young men spent two years in San Quentin prison on the basis of little more than the fact that they were of Mexican heritage. Not until October 1944, when an appeals court overturned the lower court's ruling citing lack of evidence, were they allowed to go free. The lower court's decision in the Sleepy Lagoon case reflected the stereotype among Caucasian Americans that zoot-suiters from the barrios were gang members and criminals.

Less than a year later, in June 1943, a series of race riots broke out in Los Angeles. The mayhem began when a group of sailors on leave claimed to have been attacked near the side of town occupied by Mexicans and Mexican Americans. On the nights of June 4, 5, and 6, a mob of two hundred soldiers, sailors, and marines entered the barrio and attacked Mexican youths, stripping and beating them up.

On June 7, civilians joined the servicemen in downtown Los Angeles, searching for and attacking Mexicans, Filipinos, and African Americans. The Los Angeles police took little action to stop the attacks. In the end, the Mexican government intervened, and the cancellation of military leaves finally put a stop to the carnage.

World War II. The attack, and the United States' subsequent entry into the war, provided the impetus for a rapid revival of economic activity. It was now necessary to staff the military, to set the wheels of industry rolling, to keep the nation's railroads operating, and to produce food for both the military and the home front.

The shortage of American workers meant that despite the mass deportations of recent years, there was once again a marked need for Mexican labor in the United States. In August 1942, the Mexican and US governments worked together to institute the Mexican Farm Labor Supply Program, popularly known as the bracero program.

The word bracero comes from the Spanish *brazo*, meaning "arm." These workers, most of them men, would be called upon to perform long hours of strenuous work in the fields and on the railroads. According to the agreed-upon terms of their employment, their work was to be seasonal, where applicable, and temporary—only for as long as extra hands were needed. As contract laborers, or guest workers, the braceros were to return to Mexico when their work was completed.

The guest workers of the bracero program, which was initially slated to run from 1942 to 1947, were distributed among twenty-one states but were concentrated mainly in the Southwest. Texas was the exception, by order of the Mexican government. Because of its harsh discrimination against and abusive treatment of Mexicans in the past, the Lone Star State was to receive no braceros during the war years.

The Mexican government stipulated that the braceros be paid a fair wage, given reasonable accommodations, and treated with respect. This, however, did not always happen. Wages were only about thirty cents an hour (low even for 1942), and sleeping bunks were often in converted chicken houses or abandoned railway cars. Many of the guest workers of World

War II tolerated such abysmal conditions because they were driven by desperation. Annual incomes of laborers in Mexico were so low that the braceros considered themselves fortunate to be able to earn $500 a year.

The bracero program was extended several times after 1947, and actually ran for twenty-two years, until 1964. Texas instituted a "good neighbor" policy toward Mexico and, in 1947, began to receive the much-needed contract laborers. A grower in the Lone Star State was heard to remark, "We used to own slaves but now we rent them from the government"—a reference to the terrible pay and shelter offered to these guest workers.

During the war years, about one hundred thousand braceros worked in the United States. Their number had soared to nearly five million by the time the contract worker program ended in 1964. The bracero program appears to have been a beneficial undertaking for both the United States and Mexico. However, it also vastly increased the number of undocumented immigrants from Mexico. Only about one in ten Mexican laborers was accepted into the program, so a swelling number of unsuccessful applicants crossed the border on their own and found work. These undocumented workers were often joined by braceros who had broken their contracts or had overstayed their assigned time in the United States.

The World War II years also revealed the depth of prejudice against Mexicans that prevailed in the Southwest, especially in California and Texas, and had existed for generations. Even as four hundred thousand Mexican Americans were serving in the armed forces of the United States, anti-Mexican bias was rampant in Los Angeles. The Sleepy Lagoon case and the Zoot Suit Riots of 1942 and 1943 were two examples of the shameful treatment Mexicans and Mexican Americans faced.

The Internment of Japanese Americans

While Mexican guest workers were on the whole encouraged to travel to the United States during the 1940s owing to the heavy demand for labor, the Japanese immigrants who had arrived between the 1890s and the 1920s received very different treatment.

When the United States entered World War II in 1941, it had a Japanese population of about 127,000, highly concentrated in California and other West Coast states. Most of the Japanese population consisted of families with second-generation children, engaged mainly in small businesses, farming, and fishing. The second generation, or children of immigrants, were American citizens by virtue of having been born on US soil. However, objections to the Japanese presence from nativist and anti-Asian groups, from white farming organizations, and even from public school systems, were widespread.

Using a term for Japanese people that is now considered offensive, US senator Tom Stewart exemplified the racism that many Americans directed at Asian Americans when he said, "A Jap born on our soil is a subject of Japan under Japanese law; therefore, he owes his allegiance to Japan [and should not] have a right to claim American citizenship." The senator added that "taking the oath of allegiance to this country would not help" or prove that Japanese Americans were more loyal to the United States than Japan. "They do not believe in God and have no respect for an oath," Stewart wrongfully claimed.

Many believed that Japanese Americans had been in some way responsible for Japan's surprise attack on the United States territory of Hawaii on December 7, 1941—that perhaps they were working as spies or could guide Japanese warplanes and ships to targets in Hawaii or California.

At a reception center in Los Angeles, California, in 1942, Japanese American internees wait to register.

However, there was no evidence of any such activities. What's more, there were much larger populations of people of German and Italian heritage on American soil (Germany and Italy were Japan's allies in World War II) than there were people of Japanese heritage. However, because Germans and Italians were considered to be racially white, they had been given the opportunity to become naturalized citizens, and unlike the Japanese, they were not despised and suspected of disloyalty.

Americans began to demand that every person of Japanese descent on the West Coast, whether resident alien or citizen by birth, be rounded up and incarcerated. Such outcries were so intense that only ten weeks after the Pearl Harbor attack—on February 19, 1942—President Franklin D. Roosevelt signed into law Executive Order 9066. The presidential order put the United States Army in charge of clearing so-called "military areas" of "any or all persons" for "the successful prosecution of the war."

The Japanese were not mentioned explicitly, but it soon became clear that they were the specific target of the order.

By March 1942, official posters spelling out evacuation orders began to appear in public places, instructing "all persons of Japanese ancestry living in the following areas" to prepare to leave their homes and businesses within roughly five days. They were to take with them only what they could carry—bed linens, clothing, toilet articles—but no furniture, mattresses, or kitchen equipment, and no pets. A total of 117,000 people of Japanese ancestry—two in three of whom were American-born citizens—were affected by Roosevelt's executive order.

They had to sell their homes, businesses, automobiles, and other possessions on short notice for a fraction of their worth, or otherwise leave them in the care of non-Japanese residents. Their new homes would be "relocation" camps, hastily constructed in some of the harshest and most desolate areas of the country: inland deserts, mountains, and swamps. Internees in western Washington State were forced to live in cowsheds and horse stalls for a time. As many as five families were forced to shared cramped quarters at the camps. Internees faced food shortages and poor sanitation and were surrounded by guard towers and barbed-wire fences.

Bumper stickers reading "No Japs Wanted in California" greeted the Japanese Americans returning to their homes at the close of World War II in August 1945. Houses and businesses left behind in the care of others were often found vandalized, and as no new housing had been built during the war years, some returnees found themselves once again in temporary quarters such as Quonset huts and trailers. In the cities, stores hung signs that read "No Japs Served," and in the countryside, Japanese American farmers who had reoccupied their holdings were threatened by racist vigilantes who fired shots in the night.

However, under the leadership of civic organizations and some political figures, the general public gradually began to change its attitude toward Asian Americans. In 1943, Congress had repealed the ban on Chinese immigration. As a result of the brutal aggression of Japanese forces in China during World War II, that country had become a wartime ally of the United States.

Then, in 1952, the passage of the McCarran-Walter Immigration and Naturalization Act lifted the ban on all Asian immigration and made citizenship through naturalization available to Asians. It would take a very long time, however, before the Japanese Americans who had endured prejudice, false accusations, prison-camp internment, and broken lives were compensated for their losses during World War II.

In 1976, thirty-four years after President Roosevelt signed Executive Order 9066, the evacuation decree was officially revoked. Then-president Gerald Ford called the internment one of the country's "national mistakes," declaring that "not only was the evacuation wrong, but Japanese Americans were and are loyal Americans." The issue of monetary compensation for the survivors of the camps would not be decided, however, until the Commission on Wartime Relocation and Internment of Civilians released its findings and recommendations in 1983.

Each surviving evacuee was to receive the sum of $20,000. The distribution of the monies did not take place until 1990, by which time close to half of the 117,000 internees had died. With each check that was mailed, President George H. W. Bush enclosed an official letter: "We can never fully right the wrongs of the past. But … in enacting a law calling for restitution and offering a sincere apology, your fellow Americans have … renewed their traditional commitment to the ideals of freedom, equality, and justice."

The checks to the surviving internees were distributed according to age, beginning with the eldest. First among them was wheelchair-bound Mamoru Eto, whose restitution was presented in a public ceremony. He was 107 years old.

Refugees from Hitler's Europe

Economic need and the search for a better life have long been among the factors that drove immigrants across borders and oceans to the United States. Other groups, though, have left their countries to escape religious persecution, oppressive political systems, and even life-threatening regimes.

The latter was the case for the European victims of the Nazi regime of Adolf Hitler. The majority of those threatened with the Nazi punishments of imprisonment, hard labor, torture, and death were Jews. Hitler's plan for restoring Germany's influence on the world stage after its shattering defeat in World War I included the "purification" of its population. This meant weeding out not only Jews but also Roma peoples, homosexuals, the physically imperfect, the mentally ill, and any religious leaders or other public figures who opposed Hitler. As World War II progressed and Hitler expanded Germany's territorial holdings in Europe to include Austria, Czechoslovakia, Poland, Norway, Denmark, the Netherlands, Belgium, and France, more and more people targeted by the Nazis tried to escape.

Hitler's violent campaign against the Jews began when he was appointed chancellor of Germany in 1933. He ordered the boycott of Jewish businesses and enforced his orders with the presence of Nazi storm troopers. In 1935, having gained dictatorial power in Germany, Hitler stripped Jews of their citizenship and began to take over their businesses, property, and bank accounts, punishing anyone who defied him with beatings and arrests.

The autumn of 1938 saw a massive assault on Germany's Jews. On November 9–10, countless Jewish homes, 8,000 shops, 200 synagogues, and Jewish hospitals and orphanages were vandalized, looted, and burned; 30,000 Jewish men were rounded up and sent to concentration camps. This event is known as

Kristallnacht, or "The Night of Broken Glass," because of the thousands of windows that were smashed.

Already, many of Germany's half-million Jews had fled the country, seeking refuge in the Netherlands, Belgium, Switzerland, France, Great Britain, Palestine, and even the city of Shanghai in China. The most favored destination, though, was the United States, to which many eminent scientists such as Albert Einstein, as well as famous writers, composers, and artists, had fled.

In the United States, however, the quota system as set forth in the Immigration Law of 1924 was still in effect. For each of the years of 1938 and 1939, a maximum of 27,370 immigrants from Germany were allowed entry. The quota was met for the first time in 1939, and by June of that year, more than three hundred thousand Germans had been placed on a waiting list for visas.

With regard to Kristallnacht, President Franklin Roosevelt declared, "I myself could scarcely believe that such things could occur in a twentieth-century civilization." Yet members of the president's own State Department were deeply anti-Semitic, as was much of the population of the United States throughout the 1930s. Assistant Secretary of State Breckenridge Long, who was in charge of handling refugee affairs, was notorious for his opposition to letting Jews from Hitler's Europe enter the United States. In 1941, with many Jews already consigned to Germany's death camps, Long wrote in his diary that he believed "the general type of intending immigrant was just the same as the criminal Jews who crowd our police court dockets in New York."

Even refuge-seekers who had already been assigned numbers in accordance with the quota system were subjected to waits of a year or more for entry visas. With chances for emigration from Nazi-run Germany rapidly diminishing, some of Hitler's potential victims took desperate chances for escape. Among them were 933 passengers who sailed for the Western Hemisphere in May 1939 aboard a ship called the *St. Louis*. The ship was headed

German-Jewish refugees wave from the deck of the ship *St. Louis* as they arrive in Belgium in 1939 after a journey of thousands of miles.

for Cuba, where about 2,500 refugees were already waiting for admission to the United States. However, the ship was turned away, and with nowhere to go, was eventually forced to return to Europe. The failure of the *St. Louis* to deliver its passengers to a safe haven was only one of a number of attempts by Jews and others to escape before the outbreak of World War II in September 1939.

Palestine, where many Jews had been buying land since the late 1800s, was another hoped-for destination. As a result of World War I, Palestine had become a mandate of England, which meant that this territory, with a long-established Arab population, was under British control. As an increasing number of European Jews attempted to reach the shores of what had in ancient times been their homeland, the would-be Jewish immigrants clashed with Palestinian Arabs. England subsequently closed Palestine to the boatloads of refugees arriving in leaky and unsafe vessels, forcing them to return to Hitler's Europe.

In May 1945, when World War II ended in Europe, six million Jews had been murdered by the Nazi regime. Why weren't more of them given the chance to find sanctuary in the United States while there was still time to leave Germany? Between 1933 and 1940, the total allotment of quota spaces for immigrants from Germany was 211,895. Yet, during that period only 100,987 permits to enter the United States were actually issued. This happened because of longstanding nativist concerns regarding the immigration of "hordes" of "alien" people, combined with the deep strain of anti-Semitism that infected both the nation and the world. Such discriminatory practices would continue to motivate immigration policy around the world and in the United States. While US nativists would continue to argue that such policies were necessary to maintain the cultural makeup of the country and protect American jobs, others would point to the words of Jewish American poet Emma Lazarus. These words had been inscribed on the Statue of Liberty, one of the first sights immigrants would see as they arrived by ship to Ellis Island:

> *Give me your tired, your poor,*
> *Your huddled masses yearning to breathe free,*
> *The wretched refuse of your teeming shore.*
> *Send these, the homeless, tempest-tossed, to me:*
> *I lift my lamp beside the golden door.*

THE NEW COLOSSUS

THE NEW COLOSSUS.

NOT LIKE THE BRAZEN GIANT OF GREEK FAME,
WITH CONQUERING LIMBS ASTRIDE FROM LAND TO LAND
HERE AT OUR SEA-WASHED, SUNSET GATES SHALL STAND
A MIGHTY WOMAN WITH A TORCH, WHOSE FLAME
IS THE IMPRISONED LIGHTNING, AND HER NAME
MOTHER OF EXILES. FROM HER BEACON-HAND
GLOWS WORLD-WIDE WELCOME; HER MILD EYES COMMAND
THE AIR-BRIDGED HARBOR THAT TWIN CITIES FRAME.
"KEEP ANCIENT LANDS, YOUR STORIED POMP!"
    CRIES SHE
WITH SILENT LIPS. "GIVE ME YOUR TIRED, YOUR
    POOR,
YOUR HUDDLED MASSES YEARNING TO BREATHE FREE,
THE WRETCHED REFUSE OF YOUR TEEMING SHORE.
SEND THESE, THE HOMELESS, TEMPEST-TOST TO ME,
I LIFT MY LAMP BESIDE THE GOLDEN DOOR!"

———

THIS TABLET, WITH HER SONNET TO THE BARTHOLDI STATUE
OF LIBERTY ENGRAVED UPON IT, IS PLACED UPON THESE WALLS
IN LOVING MEMORY OF

EMMA LAZARUS

BORN IN NEW YORK CITY, JULY 22d, 1849
DIED NOVEMBER 19TH, 1887.

Chapter Four

GIVE ME YOUR TIRED, YOUR POOR

By the end of World War II in 1945, millions of people in Europe found themselves unable to return to their homes. What would happen to those lives and livelihoods that had been ravaged by the atrocities of war would become a matter of debate for US lawmakers. Meanwhile, the Cold War between the United States and the Soviet Union, and political upheavals in the Caribbean, would present new immigration challenges to policymakers.

Displaced Persons

Both the fighting and the occupied nations of Europe were in states of physical destruction and social disarray

Opposite: Emma Lazarus's poem "The New Colossus" is displayed on the base of the Statue of Liberty.

by the end of the war. Towns and cities had been bombed, their public buildings, factories, and dwellings smashed and burned, and their rail lines, bridges, and highways reduced to rubble.

The human effects of this devastation were most serious. The survivors of the prisons and the death camps were free. However, many were suffering from poor health, impoverished, and largely unable to return to their homes. Families had been torn apart, entire neighborhoods had vanished, and property and financial records had disappeared. Even those who presumably had a home village or town to return to were often unwilling to try to do so, fearing a hostile reception from their former neighbors.

As a result, Europe in 1945 was inhabited by as many as two million displaced and homeless individuals. The Allied authorities—those countries such as the United Kingdom and France that had emerged victorious against Germany and its allies—and the United Nations could do little more than provide emergency shelters that were referred to as displaced persons (DP) camps.

Some of the temporary quarters were former concentration camps—where so many Jews had been interned and murdered—or army camps. Other DP housing consisted of large buildings converted into makeshift shelters in urban areas. Rehabilitation, family reunification, and starting a new life took many more than a decade. Indeed, it wasn't until the late 1950s that most of the DP camps were able to close.

Jewish DPs, who numbered about 250,000, were especially anxious to emigrate. Many sought a new home in Palestine and continued their efforts to enter it illegally between 1945 and 1948. Their goal of legal immigration was realized when the British relinquished their mandate over Palestine and the newly independent state of Israel was born on May 14, 1948.

Other DPs sought a means of entry into the United States. President Harry S. Truman—who had succeeded Franklin

Roosevelt in 1945—was deeply aware of "the homeless and suffering refugees of all faiths." As early as his January 1946 State of the Union address, Truman urged Congress to draft a Displaced Persons Act permitting the immigration of European refugees who could not be admitted under the existing quotas. No legislation was sent to Truman for his signature, however, until June 25, 1948.

Truman was so dissatisfied with the final draft of the Displaced Persons Act that he made a public statement, explaining that he was signing it under protest because the refugees could wait no longer and Congress was about to adjourn for the summer. "The bill discriminates in callous fashion against displaced persons of the Jewish faith," Truman declared, pointing to a provision that restricted the eligibility of those Jewish victims who had fled liberated camps in Poland and elsewhere to find sanctuary in the American zones of Germany, Austria, and Italy on or before December 22, 1945. The same technicality applied to displaced persons of the Catholic faith, many of whom had fled to American zones as refugees from the Communist regime imposed on Eastern Europe by the Soviet Union.

What's more, Truman pointed out, the Displaced Persons Act did not eliminate the existing quotas of national origin. The quota restrictions would be dropped only temporarily. "The bill," Truman summarized, after pointing out several other unfair and restrictive requirements, "reflects a singular lack of confidence by the Congress in the capacity and willingness of the people of the United States to extend a welcoming hand to the prospective immigrants." He termed the legislation "a bitter disappointment."

Nonetheless, the Displaced Persons Act of 1948, along with its more generous amended version of 1950, stood as the first legislated refugee program for the United States. It would result in the admission of four hundred thousand mainly European refugees, of whom eighty thousand were Jewish.

Refugees of Communism

Although the Soviet Union had fought alongside Great Britain, France, and the United States against Germany during World War II, no sooner had the peace arrangements been made than a political rift developed between the former allies.

The Soviet Union, or USSR—a giant Communist nation that sprawled across eastern Europe into Asia—claimed the spoils of its share in the Allied victory by taking political control of surrounding smaller nations in Europe and elsewhere. The United States' opposition to the spread of communist ideology and struggle with the Soviet Union on the international stage became known as the Cold War, a lengthy period of nonviolent conflict extending from the mid–1940s to 1991. The Cold War was the product of Western democracies' concern over Soviet expansionism. It ended when the Soviet Union dissolved into a number of separate and independent nations in 1991, and Russia was reborn after nearly seventy years of Soviet rule.

Fierce conflicts and deep tensions existed between the Soviets and the West. The rivalry between the United States and its wartime ally took many forms. The two nations competed militarily and industrially in areas that ranged from nuclear weapons and defense to technology and the space race. Although the United States and the Soviet Union never engaged directly in war, the American determination to contain the growth of communism led to confrontations in what were known as proxy wars.

The Cold War also spurred postwar immigration to the United States. Escapees from the Soviet Union and its satellite countries in Eastern Europe were few, owing to the harsh emigration restrictions that contained populations behind the Iron Curtain (as Britain's wartime prime minister, Winston Churchill, described the metaphorical barrier surrounding the Soviet-controlled world). When a brief uprising against Soviet rule occurred in Hungary in the 1950s, however, and when Cubans sought to leave their newly Communist-dominated island in the 1960s, the United States readily overrode the quotas that had existed since 1924 and had been reaffirmed as recently as 1952. The restrictionists of the day were inclined to be lenient toward the refugees from these conflicts because they were considered victims of America's ideological archenemy.

Cuban Refugees

The influx of Cuban refugees to the United States began in the early 1960s and continued for decades. Only 90 miles (145 km) from the Florida Keys, the Caribbean island of Cuba had become an independent nation in 1909. Until 1959, it was ruled by a series of right-wing dictators who were supported by the United States. However, starting in the 1950s, Communist rebels under

Cuban refugees wait in line at the Cuban Refugee Emergency Center in Florida in 1965 in the hopes of helping their relatives leave Cuba.

the leadership of Fidel Castro began to stage guerrilla warfare against the established government. This resulted in a revolution, with Castro becoming premier of Cuba in January 1959.

In fomenting a revolution in Cuba, Castro, a committed Marxist, had developed close ties with the Soviet Union, and his government followed the Soviet pattern of a single-party political system, a government-run economy, and the restriction of personal freedoms. Soon after Castro took over the reins in Cuba, property was seized; the sugar factories, hotels, banks, and other means of wealth owned by upper-class Cubans were nationalized; and trade and diplomatic relations between the United States and Cuba were broken off. The United States then declared a trade embargo.

Within a few years of Castro's rise to power, the Cuban-born population of the United States rose from 124,000 to more than 400,000. Most of those who initially fled Castro's regime were families of educated upper- and middle-class people trying to preserve whatever assets they could and seeking freedom of expression.

Miami, Florida, was a preferred destination for the immigrants as the exodus began. Union City, New Jersey, was another area of early Cuban settlement. Departing from its earlier pattern, the United States provided aid to the new arrivals in accordance with the passage of the Cuban Adjustment Act of 1966. Public assistance, courses in English, college scholarships and low-interest loans, financial aid, and health care were offered to the new arrivals. Banks provided business loans without collateral so that Cubans could reestablish themselves and contribute to the US economy. Politically, the Cuban exiles formed a valuable base for a growing anti-Castro movement.

A second wave of refugees from communism came through in the years between 1966 and 1974. They consisted of middle- and working-class Cubans, many transported via "freedom

Opening the Door to Hungarian Refugees

After World War II, American lawmakers continued to favor immigrants who shared similar backgrounds with the English, Dutch, and Nordic Protestants who had settled the country in the 1700s and the early 1800s. As a result, the McCarran-Walter Immigration and Naturalization Act of 1952 retained many of the features of the quota system instituted in the Immigration Law of 1924. It made naturalization possible for Asian immigrants, but the Chinese and Japanese quotas were minuscule compared to those for northern and western Europeans. The law also required intensive screening of immigrants suspected of being communists.

Soon enough, however, unrest among populations living under communism in various parts of the world made it clear that the national-origin quotas would have to be modified.

Hungary was an Eastern European country of ten million people that, along with other nations, had fallen under the control of the Soviet Union. In late October 1956, the Hungarian people rose up against the Communist regime and gained control of most of the country.

In early November, as Soviet troops and tanks began pouring across the border into Hungary, the rebels called a general strike and blew up mines and industrial installations. In the streets of the capital city, Budapest, Hungarian freedom fighters engaged in fierce gun battles with the Soviets. However, within days, the revolt was crushed, its leaders killed or sent to Soviet prison camps. Nearly two hundred thousand Hungarians sought to escape to the West.

The United States took in eighty thousand Hungarian refugees, and other nations accepted smaller numbers. Meanwhile, the Cold War persisted, while refugees and asylum-seekers continued to look for havens abroad.

flights" to the United States during a period of cooperation between the two nations. A special privilege granted in 1966 was permanent US residency after one year, paving the way to citizenship.

Stormier relations between the United States and Cuba in 1980 led to an interruption in normal immigration. Through what became known as the Mariel Boatlift, tens of thousands of mainly poor Cubans embarked from the Cuban port of Mariel in leaky and unsafe boats headed for the tip of Florida. An estimated 120,000 fleeing Cubans arrived during this period.

The collapse of the Soviet Union in the early 1990s spurred a fourth wave of Cuban refugees. As a Soviet satellite dependent on the USSR for sugar subsidies, food, gasoline, and electricity, Cuba was badly hurt by the withdrawal of this aid and went into an economic tailspin. What's more, in 1992, the United States tightened its trade embargo with Cuba. As a result, many more Cubans were thrown into poverty.

With the disintegration of the Soviet Union, the Cold War began to recede into the past, and in 1994, the United States set quota limits on Cuban immigration for the first time. No more than twenty thousand visas would be issued annually.

This restriction led almost at once to a wave of attempts to immigrate illegally. In the years since the imposition of the quota, many Cubans have tried to enter the United States from Mexico. Others have resorted to various types of sea travel, often on boats that are overcrowded and unsafe.

One variety of craft is the "go-fast" boat, a high-powered vessel that can evade the border patrol cruisers of the US Coast Guard as they surveil the waters off the shores of Florida. The smugglers who operate go-fast boats charge $6,000 to $10,000 per passenger and cram as many as seventy into a space that is meant for ten. The cost of the passage from Cuba is often paid by relatives who have already established themselves in the United States.

Such practices have resulted in tragedies at sea. Go-fast boats about to be apprehended by the US Coast Guard have been known to throw passengers overboard to distract their pursuers. The hiring of these boats became less common after the administration of President Barack Obama eliminated the so-called "wet-foot, dry-foot" policy that once applied to Cuban immigrants; according to this policy, Cubans caught at sea were sent back to Cuba, but those who made it to shore were permitted to stay.

The Case of Elián González

A complicated example of the consequences of an illegal boatlift from Cuba to Florida was seen in the case of Elián González, who was found floating at sea in the Florida Straits on an inner tube. Technically, because the young Cuban boy was found in the water, he should have been returned to Cuba. However, his age and his family circumstances led to a custody battle that made headlines in both Cuba and the United States.

Six-year-old Elián González was the child of divorced parents who lived in Cuba. In November 1999, his mother elected to leave the island in a small, aluminum boat to start a new life with her boyfriend, a smuggler who lived in Miami. She took her young son with her.

Thirteen passengers and an operator were aboard the boat when its engine failed. As the flimsy craft capsized, Elián's mother, her boyfriend, and nine others drowned. Only Elián and two other passengers—a pair of young adults—survived, rescued by fishermen, as they floated aimlessly on the inner tube.

The survivors were turned over to the Coast Guard and then to the Immigration and Naturalization Service (INS). In Miami, Elián's paternal great-uncle had already been notified by Elián's father that the boy had been taken by his mother, and that he should be returned to Cuba if found.

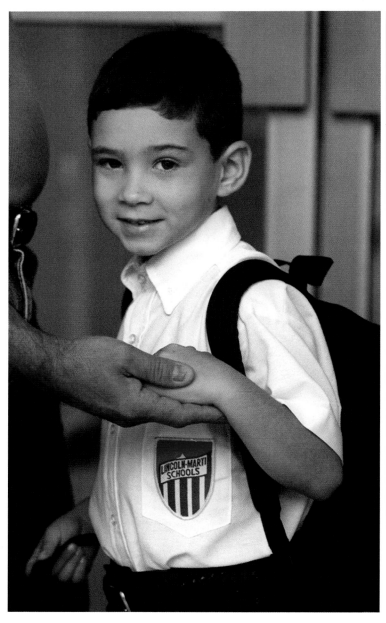

Elián González, a young Cuban refugee, attends his first day of class in the United States on January 4, 2000.

The great-uncle, Lázaro González, at first appeared to agree with the wishes of Elián's father, but once the child was temporarily placed in his care, Lázaro and his immediate family, along with a vocal segment of the anti-Castro Cuban community, began to advocate for permanent residency and even instant citizenship by an act of Congress for Elián. Months of public demonstrations, media coverage, and video of Elián being showered with Christmas gifts and taken to Disney World followed—as did legal and political disputes. Civic leaders and local police vowed to prevent federal authorities from removing Elián to be reunited with his father. Confused and prompted by his Miami relatives, the boy spoke to his father, Juan Miguel, by telephone and expressed a desire to remain in the United States.

Meanwhile, the INS interviewed Juan Miguel and determined that he was a caring and emotionally involved father, and the appropriate person to speak for Elián. The Miami relatives were still trying to get court orders to grant Elián asylum (special refugee permission outside of conventional immigration law to remain in the country) when US Attorney General Janet Reno set an April 2000 deadline for Elián's removal from their home.

On the morning of April 22, heavily armed agents of the US Border Patrol entered the Miami house and—as several hundred protesters threw rocks and bottles, burned tires and trash bins, and erected road blocks—transported Elián to a US Air Force base. There he was reunited with his father, who had been flown in from Cuba.

It was not until June 28, 2000, that Elián and his father returned home to Cuba. Persistent in their demand that Elián should remain in the United States—and backed by a number of high-ranking politicians—the Miami family had appealed to the Supreme Court for a ruling. In the end, though, the nation's highest court refused to review a lower court's decision that Elián was too young to file for asylum. The case of the child who had miraculously survived an illegal boatlift operation had revealed deep divisions that reached all the way to the Capitol.

Haitian Asylum-Seekers

Haitians also sought asylum in the United States from oppressive political regimes during the twentieth century, but they met with a very different reception than those fleeing Hungary and Cuba. Haiti is on the Caribbean island of Hispaniola, which it shares with the Dominican Republic.

Haiti declared its independence from France in 1804. Since then, conditions of extreme underdevelopment and poverty combined with gang violence and political turmoil have made Haiti one of the poorest nations on earth. Its population of just over 10.6 million is 95 percent black (descendants of African slaves who worked on sugar plantations) but has historically been ruled by an elite minority of mulattos (people with mixed white and black heritage).

The first large outflow of Haitian refugees came in the 1960s, during the long reign of "president for life" François Duvalier, commonly known as Papa Doc. Impressively educated and holding a medical degree, Papa Doc succeeded a number of short-lived, American-installed Haitian presidents and took office in 1957.

Clever, corrupt, and militarily powerful, Duvalier terrified the population through his secret police, known as the Tontons Macoutes. *Tontons Macoutes* translates loosely into "uncle bogeymen"; they were named after a mythical Haitian demon that snatches people and makes them disappear forever. In his relations with the United States, Papa Doc played a two-faced game, receiving loans with false promises to work politically against the Communism of the recently installed Castro regime in Cuba. However, it was the chaotic internal scene in Haiti—a hungry and homeless lower class oppressed by the government

François Duvalier, popularly known as Papa Doc, was a brutal and corrupt Haitian dictator.

via uniformed thugs—that led to the first of many outflows of desperate emigrants.

The earliest escapees from the Duvalier regime in the 1960s were members of the limited professional class, mainly doctors and educators, who could obtain visas for the United States under the existing quota. They were soon followed by large numbers of the impoverished, who quickly exceeded the limits set for legal immigration from Haiti at the time. These largely unskilled Haitians fell into the category of refugees whose last recourse was to become asylum-seekers. The United Nations has defined a refugee as a person who cannot return to his or her country because of "a well-founded fear of persecution for reasons of race, religion, nationality, membership in a particular social group, or political opinion."

While some undocumented immigrants arriving from Cuba in makeshift boats were being automatically granted asylum under the "wet-foot, dry-foot" policy, the same was not true for Haitian immigrants. Throughout the fourteen-year rule of Papa Doc Duvalier, many Haitian asylum-seekers arriving on American shores were either sent back to Haiti at once or detained for varying periods under prisonlike conditions. In denying or delaying the asylum claims of the Haitians who arrived by boat, US immigration authorities asserted that many who claimed to be escaping government oppression were actually seeking a way out of poverty. Untold numbers who attempted the 600-mile (966 km) ocean voyage were either apprehended by the US Coast Guard and returned to Haiti or drowned at sea in flimsy vessels.

Conditions for Haitians did not improve with the death of Papa Doc in 1971. Duvalier had groomed his son, Jean-Claude, known as Baby Doc, to succeed him. The nineteen-year-old heir continued in his father's footsteps, stealing Haiti's public funds, imprisoning and torturing his enemies, and crushing the citizenry.

Haitians continued to flee throughout Baby Doc's fifteen years in power, mostly by hazardous and often fatal sea journeys. In 1986, the younger Duvalier was removed from office through a popular uprising and exiled to France. Succeeding leaders have been less brutal than the Duvaliers. However, factional infighting has driven several from office, and political unrest has continued.

Haitian immigrants have had a more difficult time being accepted in the United States than have Cubans and other Caribbean island peoples. They are often discriminated against because of both their race and their language: Haitian creole is a mixture of French and certain African tongues. Today, nearly seven hundred thousand Haitian immigrants live in the United States, mainly in South Florida and in New York City. They range from professionals to middle- and working-class people, and many have established businesses.

A comparison of these groups of immigrants from very different places—post–World War II Europe, Cuba, and Haiti—reveals how questions of race, ethnicity, and national origin play out in both political and social arenas. Such dynamics still drive immigration policy today.

Chapter Five

CHANGING PATTERNS OF IMMIGRATION

The end of World War II brought survivors of the Nazi death machine and displaced Europeans to the United States. The Cold War brought escapees from Soviet-dominated Hungary and Communist Cuba. However, further changes were soon to come. During the 1960s, when about 320,000 documented immigrants entered the United States per year, 40 percent of them were Europeans. By the 1990s, with 900,000 documented new arrivals annually (nearly three times more than in the 1960s), only 13 percent were from Europe. This trend has continued into the present.

Revising Immigration Policy

What has accounted for the changing composition of America's newcomers, bringing many more

Opposite: Standing before the Statue of Liberty on October 3, 1965, President Lyndon B. Johnson gives a speech before signing the Immigration and Nationality Act.

Asians and Latin Americans than Europeans, to the United States? Many factors were at play. One of them was the United States' position as a political and industrial world power, regarded with awe from abroad, especially by the politically oppressed and the economically deprived.

The 1960s in the United States was also the civil rights era, during which much of the nation came to regard social justice and equality among the races as important goals. It no longer seemed fair to show preferences to certain countries over others through the national-origin quotas based on population size set by the McCarran-Walter Immigration and Naturalization Act of 1952 and by its forerunner, the Immigration Law of 1924.

So, in 1965, during the administration of President Lyndon Johnson and with the strong support of Senator Ted Kennedy of Massachusetts, the US Congress passed the Immigration and Nationality Act of 1965, also known as the Hart-Celler Act.

The original intention of the new law was to equalize immigration opportunities by issuing a fixed number of 20,000 visas per nation per year to countries in the Eastern Hemisphere and setting a ceiling of 170,000 immigrants per year. (The Western Hemisphere was allowed 120,000 immigrants per year, but the 20,000-per-country limit was not applied until 1976.)

Other provisions of the 1965 law included the sponsorship of family members from abroad by US citizens and permanent residents in the interest of family reunification. Unmarried children younger than twenty-one, husbands and wives, and parents could now be admitted to the country outside the quota system. Preferences under the quota system were given to sisters and brothers and their spouses and to other close relatives, leading to what would become known as "chain immigration." Other preference categories under the quota went to professionals, scientists, and artists "of exceptional ability," to employees in occupations with labor shortages, and to political refugees.

Unforeseen by the supporters of the Immigration and Nationality Act of 1965 was its influence on racial diversity in the United States. In 1965, prior to the act's passage, the nation's population was 89 percent white and the only minority of any significant size were African Americans, who comprised 10 percent of the population. Today, Hispanics and Latinos are the largest minority—some 17.8 percent of the population. African Americans make up about 13.3 percent. Asians are the third-largest nonwhite racial group at 5.7 percent. As a result, the steadily shrinking proportion of white Americans who are not Hispanic or Latino was 61.3 percent according to the 2016 census.

This change came about largely as the result of the Immigration and Nationality Act of 1965. The law was primarily intended to equalize immigration opportunities for all ethnic European groups. However, as Europe entered a period of postwar prosperity, its people saw little advantage in leaving their countries of birth. By the mid-1960s, only those Eastern Europeans who lived in the Soviet Union or its satellite nations were anxious to emigrate, and they were shut in behind the Iron Curtain.

On the other hand, Asians now had a broader opportunity than ever before in the twentieth century to move to the United States. Qualified immigrants from the Caribbean and from the northern parts of Latin America also availed themselves of the new possibilities. Along with the opportunities the law offered for family reunification, the introduction of these two streams of Asian and Caribbean immigrants meant that America's nonwhite population would continue to grow in unprecedented fashion.

Compare, for example, the roughly eight million European immigrants of the years 1901–1910 with the one million of 2001–2006. Compare the burgeoning numbers of Hispanic immigrants to America today with the 250,000 who arrived in 1910 in the beginning years of the so-called Great Migration.

Refugees from Vietnam and China

During the Cold War, the United States fought a major proxy war in Southeast Asia as part of its campaign to contain communism. The Vietnam War, which lasted from 1959 to 1975, took the lives of fifty-eight thousand Americans and at least three million Vietnamese militants and civilians.

The Vietnam War was a failed attempt to keep non-Communist South Vietnam from falling under the political influence of Communist North Vietnam, which had in turn

Refugees from areas north of Saigon, Vietnam, crowd onto US Navy barges in 1975, at the height of the Vietnam War.

been influenced by its powerful neighbor, the People's Republic of China. The fighting was waged ruthlessly by both sides, but the United States used massive bombing runs, and there were millions of civilian deaths. North Vietnam ultimately triumphed.

Following the cessation of hostilities, a chaotic situation ensued. Vietnamese citizens who had been government officials or military officers, or who had worked for the Americans as translators or in other capacities, were among the most threatened as the former South Vietnam was incorporated into the Communist North Vietnam under a single government. People in this category, numbering about 135,000 including family members, were the first to flee their homeland for resettlement in the United States. They were flown to military bases in California, Arkansas, Pennsylvania, and Florida, which served as reception centers until people could be resettled. Sponsors in communities around the country provided the refugees with housing and an initial means of support.

Thousands of other South Vietnamese political and military personnel, including former US government employees, were unable to leave and were sent to "re-education" camps where they were treated harshly and held in prisonlike conditions, often for years. Meanwhile, hundreds of thousands of ordinary citizens suspected of disloyalty to the new Communist regime were imprisoned in Vietnam. Others suffering as a result of political reforms and experiencing economic hardship attempted to leave the country, mainly by boat. Among them were members of a merchant class, long established in Vietnam, consisting of ethnic Chinese, as well as Vietnamese farmers and fishermen. Their attempts to reach places of refuge such as Thailand, Malaysia, Indonesia, the Philippines, and Hong Kong resulted in numerous deaths at sea in overloaded and foundering craft.

The passage of the Refugee Act of 1980 did much to facilitate South Vietnamese immigration to the United States, often

Refugee Chinese and the *Golden Venture*

The *Golden Venture* was a tramp steamer that, early in 1993, set sail from Thailand for the United States. Aboard were 286 undocumented Chinese passengers. Each passenger was said to have paid smugglers about $30,000 for the trip.

The passengers were seeking freedom from the restrictions of Communist rule. To prevent excessive population growth, China had

The *Golden Venture* is pictured where it ran ashore on a beach near New York City in 1993.

implemented a one-child policy in the late 1970s and early 1980s. Under the program, the vast majority of Chinese families were limited to no more than one child each. Couples who violated the one-child policy were threatened, or faced forcible abortions and sterilizations. In 1989, the administration of President George H. W. Bush established a new category for immigrants making asylum claims of this kind. They were termed "reproductive refugees."

One *Golden Venture* passenger, Dong Yishen, described his life as follows: "[If] your first child is a girl, the government won't argue too much if you have a second child after five years. But my second one was also a girl. In China, we really want to have a son." When Dong's wife finally gave birth to a son, the boy had to be sent to live with a childless couple. After several years, no longer able to bear the separation, Dong admitted to being the father of his third child. The authorities punished him by knocking down his house and forcing him and his family to flee.

The journey from Thailand was slow and hazardous. On June 6, 1993, the ship finally reached the coastal waters off New York City's Rockaway Beach, where it ran aground. Ten of the passengers, determined to make land, tried to swim ashore and lost their lives. The Immigration and Naturalization Service took the survivors into custody.

Most were sent to a prison for immigrant detainees in Pennsylvania, some for as long as four years. In the long run, about half the arrivals were deported and only about 10 percent were granted asylum.

through family reunification policies. Many children fathered by American soldiers during the war years in Vietnam can be counted among those admitted on this basis.

Today, immigrant Southeast Asians from Vietnam as well as from neighboring Cambodia and Laos number nearly two million. Nearly half the Vietnamese who fled to the United States following the south's defeat settled in the state of California. Diplomatic and other relations with a reunified Vietnam and with China were gradually resumed after the war.

The passage of the Immigration and Nationality Act of 1965 ushered in a new phase of Chinese immigration to the United States as well. Gone were the days of the late 1800s when California received tens of thousands of Chinese laborers working mainly in the mines and on the railroads, culminating in the Chinese Exclusion Act of 1882.

Not until 1943, when China had become an ally of the United States during World War II, was the ban on Chinese immigration repealed by Congress. The number of Chinese that might actually be admitted to the US was negligible, however. Even after the passage of the McCarran-Walter Act of 1952 (eliminating race as a bar to immigration and naturalization) the national-origin quota for China was a mere twenty thousand. So the opportunity to leave the turmoil-ridden country, still in the throes of its Communist revolution, was extremely limited. With the beginning of a stable relationship between the United States and Communist China in 1972, the trickle of Chinese from the mainland, from the island of Taiwan, and from Hong Kong began to grow.

As time went on, the twenty thousand visas available to Chinese immigrants quickly became inadequate in number. Legal immigration snowballed into illegal immigration, bringing as many as eighty thousand undocumented Chinese to the United States each year throughout the 1990s. Illegal entrance into the United States from China has taken place by various means, such as overstaying a visit or work-permit visa, jumping ship, or being smuggled into the country by Chinese crime syndicates that charge as much as $50,000 per person. The syndicates, generally known as Triads, dangerously overload crude seagoing vessels and, after landing, keep track of the passengers to collect debts owed on the passage.

Between the end of World War II in 1945 and today, the number of displaced persons and asylum-seekers seeking to enter the United States has continued to grow. In addition to European war refugees, Cubans fleeing Castro, Haitians escaping from the Duvaliers, and anti-Communist Vietnamese and Chinese, many other aliens have sought refuge in the United States. They include Afghans and Somalis, Iranians and Ethiopians, Roma people, Nicaraguans, Colombians, Dominicans, and other inhabitants of the Americas. Some are fleeing civil wars, some religious, ethnic, or political persecution, some poverty and starvation. All are seeking the opportunity for a better life.

Because only a small percentage of asylum claims are honored, and because waiting lists for visas grow longer and longer, illegal immigration has grown too. The passage of the Illegal Immigration Reform and Immigrant Responsibility Act (IIRAIRA) of 1996, which established income tests for immigrants' family members and barred future legal admission for many deportees, contributed to the influx of undocumented immigrants. The 1996 act permits even legal residents to be deported for various crimes.

Today, those seeking refuge and asylum in the United States face new challenges. Donald Trump made immigration reform one of his primary talking points on the campaign trail, and when he entered office in early 2017, he began to seek funding for a wall on the US-Mexico border. What's more, in the name of preventing terrorism, he also sought to return to nation-specific regulations that were characteristic of US immigration policy before 1965—and that, many claim, classify immigrants by race just as those earlier laws did.

Chapter Six

RECENT IMMIGRATION DEBATES

A poll of more than twelve hundred American voters in January 2018 found that 89 percent believed that legal immigration is beneficial to the United States. What's more, diversity is important to Americans: 78 percent said that immigration from diverse countries is good for the United States, and 76 percent said that, when it comes to deciding who should be allowed to immigrate to the United States, country of origin shouldn't be a factor.

Still, policies targeting people from specific countries are returning as one proposed method to control immigration. The debate over whether a US-Mexico border wall should be built has heated up under President Donald Trump, a strong proponent for such

Opposite: Newly inaugurated US president Donald Trump signs an executive order on January 27, 2017, to ban immigration from seven Muslim-majority countries for a ninety-day period.

a wall. Meanwhile, immigration raids at places of employment suspected of hiring undocumented workers continue to spark controversy. While most people seem to agree that the United States' approach to immigration today is ineffective, it remains to be seen what policies will ultimately fall into place.

Country-Specific Immigration Policy

In January 2018, during a meeting with congressional lawmakers, President Donald Trump reportedly asked why the United States would accept immigrants from Haiti and African countries, rather than encouraging more immigration from such countries as Norway. The president was broadly criticized for apparently preferring immigrants from predominantly white countries (as in the case of Norway) over predominantly black countries. Many alleged that his and similar approaches to immigration are unfairly based on the immigrant's race, religion, or country of origin.

President Trump faced similar criticism when, on January 27, 2017, he signed an executive order titled "Protecting the Nation from Foreign Terrorist Entry into the United States." The order banned citizens from seven countries with Muslim-majority populations from entering the United States for a 90-day period. The same order also prevented refugees from entering the country for a 120-day period and banned refugees from the embattled country of Syria indefinitely. Directly after the order, there was widespread confusion as thousands of travelers were detained, prevented from taking planned flights to the United States, and separated from their families. Protesters converged on airports around the country, chanting "Let them in!" The American Civil Liberties Union and many others called the policy a "Muslim ban."

The next day, a federal court blocked the order, arguing that it likely violated immigrants' rights to equal protection and due process under the US Constitution. In the decision, Judge Ann M. Donnelly of the Eastern District of New York added: "There is imminent danger that, absent the stay of removal, there will be substantial and irreparable injury to refugees, visa-holders, and other individuals." However, rather than fight this and other court orders, Trump issued a new version on March 6. The revised version had a narrowed scope, applying only to people who did not yet have valid visas. This version, too, was challenged and subsequently blocked, and a third version of the order was issued on September 24.

Trump and his supporters have defended the ban. "To be clear, this is not a Muslim ban, as the media is falsely reporting," Trump said in defense of his January 2017 order. "This is not about religion—this is about terror and keeping our country safe. There are over 40 different countries worldwide that are majority Muslim that are not affected by this order." In September 2017, Trump administration lawyers made much the same argument, insisting that the ban was motivated by a desire to protect national security.

Challenges to the ban alleged that it unfairly targeted people of a specific religion—Islam—and broadly stereotyped them as associated with terrorists. In fact, the vast majority of Muslims are peaceful, upstanding citizens, and Muslims around the globe are among the most victimized by terrorists. They pointed to a statement issued by the Trump campaign on December 7, 2015, which read: "Donald J. Trump is calling for a total and complete shutdown of Muslims entering the United States until our country's representatives can figure out what is going on." Opponents to the ban have used this statement in court as evidence that it in fact targeted a religious group—Muslims. Many have argued that it violates the establishment clause of the US Constitution, which prohibits the government from preferring any religion over another. The Trump administration, however, has pointed out that these countries were already considered high-risk during the Barack Obama administration.

On December 4, 2017, the Supreme Court allowed the ban to take full effect while challenges to the policy continued to make their way through the court system. In its latest iteration, it permitted the country to deny visas to people from six Muslim-majority countries, in addition to North Korea and Venezuela. Chad was removed from the list of banned countries in April 2018. That same month, the Supreme Court held hearings about the ban.

States and Communities

In December 2006, Immigration and Customs Enforcement (ICE) raided the Swift & Company meatpacking plant in Greeley, Colorado, rounding up 261 allegedly undocumented immigrants. Arrests and deportations followed. In some cases, the American-born children of undocumented parents were left behind with relatives. Other deportees took their children out of school and back to their native country with them to avoid the emotional hardship of parent-child separation.

Other families were permitted to remain in Greeley after the ICE raid but were forbidden to work. Tom Selders, the then-mayor of Greeley, had two hundred families in his city with no income. "Approximately $200,000 generously donated by local churches, Swift & Company, and individuals was distributed to help families pay for rent, food, and utilities," Selders recalled.

That was early in 2007. A few years later, the needs continued but the money had run out. The once-popular Republican mayor was voted out of office as a result of his criticism of the tactics

After a raid on the Swift & Company meat processing plant in Greeley, Colorado, in 2006, family members of those arrested face ICE agents.

ICE used in the raid. "People with leg irons and handcuffs—was that really necessary?" Selders asked in a *Denver Post* interview in January 2008.

"We need solutions," he continued. "People are here as a result of a failed federal policy. We can't deport 12 million people. There's not the political will. In Colorado, what would that do to our tourist industry? What would that do to our agriculture?"

Greeley's former mayor is one of numerous state and local officials who have taken the undocumented immigrant issue into their own hands. Following the devastation wrought by Katrina, the hurricane that severely damaged the Gulf Coast in 2005, the city of New Orleans welcomed immigrant labor, which turned out to be vital to its rebuilding efforts. Some states have issued

During his time as ICE acting director, Thomas D. Homan oversaw amplified deportation efforts.

driver's licenses to undocumented persons as a means of registering and identifying them.

In recent years, lawmakers in the state of California have been particularly outspoken in favor of a more progressive immigration policy. Trump and his attorney general, Jeff Sessions, have threatened to withdraw federal grant money from states and cities with so-called sanctuary laws, policies that, in various ways,

discourage local law enforcement from enforcing immigration law—which, as federal law, they are not legally required to enforce. As Dara Lind points out in *Vox*, "A lot of police chiefs think it's a net *negative* for local cops to enforce immigration law—it makes immigrant communities afraid of police and less likely to report crimes or cooperate with investigations in, say, murder cases."

In 2017, California enacted sanctuary regulations in spite of these warnings from Trump and Sessions. One of these was the California Values Act, which imposes limits on the information about minor criminals or suspected criminals that state and local law enforcement can share with federal officers. In retaliation, ICE acting director Thomas D. Homan said that California would soon see "a lot more deportation officers," adding: "We've got to start charging some of these politicians with crimes." In May 2018, the Trump administration filed a lawsuit against California, its governor, and its attorney general over these laws. The suit argued that they "reflect a deliberate effort by California to obstruct the United States' enforcement of federal immigration law."

California State Senate leader Kevin de León responded to federal criticism of the laws: "The administration is just angry that a state has stood up to them—one that embraces diversity and inclusivity and is the sixth-largest economy in the

Elvira Arellano, an Immigration Activist

Elvira Arellano, born in 1975 in the Mexican state of Michoacán, entered the United States illegally in 1997. She was deported but soon returned, and in 1999 gave birth to a son, who was a citizen by virtue of having been born on American soil.

In 2006, Elvira Arellano and Saul, her seven-year-old son, sought refuge in a Chicago church as they faced deportation to Mexico.

At the time of the terrorist attacks of September 11, 2001, Arellano was working as a cleaning woman at Chicago's O'Hare International Airport. During a nationwide investigation of airport personnel for security purposes in 2002, Arellano was apprehended, arrested, and found to be using a false Social Security card.

To avoid a 2006 court hearing that would have ordered her deportation and separated her from her son, Saul, Arellano took refuge with the boy in a Chicago church, Amor de Dios United Methodist, whose pastor had inaugurated a sanctuary movement for immigrants. Following their stay there, the Arellano family moved to another Chicago church, Adalberto United Methodist, where they remained for a year.

As an advocate for child welfare and women's rights, Arellano was president of La Familia Latina Unida (the United Latino Family), a lobbying group fighting family separation caused by deportation. In August 2007, she defied her existing deportation order by leaving her sanctuary and flying to Los Angeles to make speaking appearances and to attend rallies on behalf of family unification.

Arellano was immediately arrested and escorted to Tijuana, Mexico, by US government agents. Although eight-year-old Saul was permitted to visit his mother soon after in Mexico, Arellano said she preferred that he return to Chicago to attend school while she continued to advocate for immigrant rights.

In 2014, Arellano was legally permitted to return to the United States. Three years later, she was still awaiting a hearing regarding her request for political asylum. She argued that her life was in danger in Mexico as a result of her advocacy for better treatment of the many Central Americans who pass through Mexico on their way to the United States. In 2017, her son, Saul, graduated from high school in Chicago.

world thanks to the hard-working immigrants who want to become American citizens."

Raids and Deportations

ICE agents have indeed struck back against sanctuary laws in a series of raids on employers in California. In early 2018, the *San Francisco Chronicle* reported that ICE had raided seventy-seven Northern California businesses over a period of three days—an "unprecedented" number, according to one Los Angeles immigration attorney. In such raids, ICE demands that businesses prove that they confirmed their employees' right to work in the United States before hiring them. Proof generally comes in the form of a valid Social Security card or other identification.

A few weeks later, 212 undocumented immigrants were arrested in a five-day sweep of 122 businesses in Southern California. ICE reported that it was specifically targeting "individuals who pose a threat to national security, public safety and border security," and that of those who were arrested, 88 percent were convicted criminals. Eric Garcetti, mayor of Los Angeles, expressed his opposition to this approach to immigration: "Angelenos [people who live in Lose Angeles] should not have to fear raids that bring unnecessary anxiety to our homes, schools, and workplaces."

Homan, however, insisted that ICE had every right to conduct such raids: "Because sanctuary jurisdictions like Los Angeles prevent ICE from arresting criminal aliens in the secure confines of a jail, our officers are forced to conduct at-large arrests in the community, putting officers, the general public, and the aliens at greater risk and increasing the incidents of collateral arrests."

Nativists and immigration restrictionists generally maintain that anyone who has entered the country illegally, either by overstaying a visa or by sneaking across a border, has committed a criminal act and must be returned to his or her country of residence. In 2005, an immigration bill that sought to charge such individuals with a felony, preventing them from ever becoming citizens, passed the House of Representatives but ultimately failed to become law. Another failed bill represented a different approach. In May 2006, the Senate voted down a proposal to deport all undocumented immigrants who had been in the United States for less than two years. Those with longer residency would have been allowed to remain, with the prospect of becoming citizens.

New and more complicated provisions were put forward in another Senate bill in May 2007. This legislation would have allowed undocumented immigrants to work in the United States while applying for renewable four-year visas. The head of the household, however, would have to return to the family's home country to file an application (that is, "Get to the end of the line"), and fines would be imposed for noncompliance.

Not surprisingly, there were vigorous complaints from those who opposed giving undocumented persons a chance to attain legal status. Among those who saw such measures as "amnesty," or forgiveness of criminal action, were Colorado's anti-immigration Republican congressman Tom Tancredo and television anchor Lou Dobbs. The bill failed.

Under President Barack Obama, enforcement of immigration law was focused on deporting two primary groups: criminals, and those who had recently crossed the border without authorization. According to the Department of Homeland Security, 85 percent of people deported during fiscal year 2016 had illegally crossed the border; of the remaining deportees, 90 percent had been convicted of serious crimes. According to the Migration Policy Institute, President Obama was criticized by both the immigrant-rights and the enforcement-first communities. That's because, while the overall number of deportations decreased during the Obama years compared to the George W. Bush and Bill Clinton administrations, there were fewer people crossing the border in the first place. This has been attributed to both economic improvements in Mexico and fewer jobs in the United States after the 2007–2009 recession, among other factors.

Victims of the War in Iraq

In March 2003, the United States, under the leadership of then-president George W. Bush, undertook the invasion of the Middle Eastern nation of Iraq. He called the initiative Operation Iraqi Freedom. Claims that Iraqi president Saddam Hussein had weapons of mass destruction that he intended to use against the United States proved to be unfounded and untrue.

In the aftermath of the invasion, a state of civil war developed between and within the country's two major Muslim denominations. More than four thousand American soldiers were killed and nearly 32,000 wounded. Later, terrorist militants from a violent group that called itself the Islamic State took advantage of disarray within the country to seek political control, and left many dead in their wake. While the number of Iraqis killed as a result of Operation Iraqi Freedom has generated a great deal of controversy, an op-ed published on the Truthout website in 2018 estimated that 2.4 million had died since 2003. Earlier, more conservative estimates have placed the Iraqi death toll in the hundreds of thousands.

Violence in Iraq resulting from the American invasion led to the displacement of millions of Iraqis (of a prewar population of 24 million). In 2013, the BBC reported that

A group of Iraqi and Syrian refugee families are among 150 refugees invited to take a free guided tour of Manhattan in 2017.

nearly 2.7 million had abandoned their homes, half of them seeking refuge inside Iraq, the other half fleeing primarily to neighboring countries, such as Syria, Jordan, Iran, Egypt, and Lebanon, where they were not permitted to work and, in many cases, lived as outcasts.

Nearly 6 million people were displaced during the conflict with the Islamic State. By the end of 2017, with that organization nearly vanquished on Iraqi soil, 3.2 million people had returned home, but 2.6 million were still displaced, according to the United Nations Migration Agency.

Not unlike the refugees of the war in Vietnam, many of whom had worked for and with the Americans, or whose lives were otherwise threatened by their wartime adversaries, fleeing Iraqis sought above all to find sanctuary in the United States. Among the families held in detention at the prisonlike Texas facility known as Hutto was the family of an Iraqi named Salwan Komo. Despite having close relatives with legal status living in the United States, Komo, his wife, and their baby daughter were confined in Hutto for more than five months.

As Christians in the chaos of postinvasion Iraq, the Komos had been at the mercy of extremists who misrepresented Islam as intolerant toward people of other faiths. Family members who had fled to Syria had been unable to find work and saw their savings draining away. So the Komos, unable to obtain refugee status, attempted to enter the United States by way of Mexico. They had openly presented their case at the border and requested asylum. Instead, they found themselves at Hutto.

The Komos were among the very few Iraqis who were eventually able to resettle in the United States. In 2006, only 202 Iraqis were admitted. For the year 2007, the promised target was 7,000, but only 1,608 Iraqi refugees were allowed into the country. However, by 2016, the number of Iraqi immigrants had increased significantly to 222,000; in fact, more immigrants were coming from Iraq than from any other Middle Eastern or North African country.

Among Western nations, Sweden, with a population of nine million, opened its door to approximately 20,000 Iraqi refugees in 2007. This number becomes all the more impressive in comparison to the 1,608 Iraqis accepted in the same year by the United States, a country of more than three hundred million people at the time.

Iraqis and Afghanis who worked for the US government during the wars in Iraq and Afghanistan during the first two decades of the twenty-first century are eligible for special immigrant visas, since helping the United States was likely to have endangered them and their families. The United States has been criticized for not doing enough to protect these workers; the special visa program didn't start until 2007. Since then, the Pew Research Center reports, more than seventy thousand visas have been issued, with two in three going to Afghans. The original Trump-issued travel ban had included immigrants from Iraq, but the March 2017 revision removed Iraq from the list of countries.

Debating a Border Wall

During his campaign and his first year as US president, Donald Trump was a vocal advocate for building a border wall between the United States and Mexico. Such a wall, he said, would decrease undocumented immigration and the crimes associated with it, and would therefore be a boon to national security. But where did the idea of a wall originate, and what are the pros and cons of this type of approach to immigration?

The years 1993–1994 saw the completion of the first major border-fencing project. The triple-layer, welded-steel and wire-mesh fence between Tijuana, Mexico, and San Diego, California, is 10 feet (3 meters) high and 14 miles (16 km) long.

In the years immediately following its construction, the fence proved effective, but only to a degree. Some 450,000 undocumented immigrants had entered the California area annually before 1994; by 2002, the number was down to 100,000. During the same period, illegal crossings leapt by 342 percent in the area of Tucson, Arizona, where the border was unfenced but harsh desert terrain and extreme heat made the crossing hazardous, even life-threatening.

American vigilante groups on the Arizona border sprang into action. In April 2005, a volunteer patrol known as the Minuteman Project set up a border watch to prevent what they termed the illegal invasion of their state by undocumented Mexicans.

According to the Anti-Defamation League, some members of the group of about 150 were armed and joined by "right-wing extremists ranging from militia groups to white supremacist

A border fence divides Nogales, Mexico, from Nogales, Arizona.

organizations." These included the neo-Nazi National Alliance, which proclaimed that the Hispanic "invasion" would cause white people to be "a minority within the next 50 years."

Private citizens in Arizona also took border patrol duty into their own hands. A notorious example was Roger Barnett who, with his brother Donald, allegedly hunted illegal aliens on the thousands of acres of ranchland that Roger leased from the state. Cases reported between 1999 and 2006 indicated that the two brandished guns, fired shots, and sicced dogs on crossers. Roger Barnett claimed to have captured twelve thousand violators of the law, whom he says he turned over to the US Border Patrol.

In 2006, the federal government stepped in with the passage by Congress of the Secure Fence Act. It authorized 700 miles (1,127 km) of new fencing to be built along the Arizona and Texas borders with Mexico. As the construction of the fence, 12 to 15 feet (3.6 to 4.6 m) in height, proceeded during 2008, objections were aired by landowners, local Native American tribes, and environmentalists. Ranchers in Texas resisted fencing that would cut them off from agricultural lands along the Rio Grande. Native American communities feared that hunting areas would be lost. Wildlife groups protested that the habitats of rare fauna such as jaguars and pygmy owls would be disrupted.

Nonetheless, the fence was completed at a cost of approximately $2.8 million per mile. It consisted of various types of barriers, including chain link, sheet piling, and concrete. Still, according to Trump, this fence was not enough. Instead, he advocated for a new 1,000-mile (1,609 km) wall, which the *MIT Technological Review* has estimated could cost up to $40 billion. President Trump signed an executive order calling for such a wall shortly after his January 2017 inauguration, declaring it necessary for "the prevention of all unlawful entries into the United States, including entries by terrorists, other unlawful aliens, instruments of terrorism, narcotics, and other contraband." However, just more than $1 billion had been allotted for the construction of the wall by early 2018—funding that Trump called a down payment on the project.

Some argue that a border wall would be both prohibitively expensive and relatively ineffective. "We can spend billions of dollars to build a 10-foot wall on top of a 10,000-foot mountain," said Jeh Johnson, former secretary of the Department of Homeland Security, "but if you've come all the way from Central America, it's not going to stop you." Many point to the US Border Patrol's currently active "digital wall" of about eight thousand cameras, eleven thousand sensors, eight drones, and other resources as a more effective approach.

Chapter Seven

CULTURAL AND ECONOMIC DEBATES

It can sometimes seem hard to believe that anyone on either side of the immigration debate in the United States could change their opinion. By early 2018, the American public appeared largely divided into two camps with very little in common. To reach a more nuanced understanding of the many factors contributing to these and other points of view on US immigration today, it is necessary to understand a few final arguments.

Extreme Views on Both Sides

Extreme perspectives regarding both legal and illegal immigration continue to exist in the United States.

Opposite: Migrant farm workers in North Carolina count their chips, each of which represents a single basket of harvest, and each of which earns them one dollar.

Some nativists and restrictionists take the view that America's white Protestant past has been sullied by waves of newcomers from eastern and southern Europe, from Asia, and from Latin America, among other places. Their chief argument regarding immigrants comprises three elements. Geographically, they say, the United States is no longer a broad frontier open to settlement from abroad. Economically, immigrants are said to threaten the well-being of the US workforce and increase the tax burden on the entire population. Culturally, immigrants alter the traditional American way of life by introducing different lifestyles and languages to the nation. Many also assume that immigrants tend to be lawbreakers, and that even among legal entrants there is a moral laxness that does not conform to the norms of behavior that supposedly existed among Americans of an earlier time. This last assertion is exemplified by then-candidate Donald Trump's statement that, "When Mexico sends its people ... They're bringing drugs. They're bringing crime."

An extremist view at the opposite end of the spectrum sees all immigrants as passive victims of human exploitation, both in their home countries and in their new settings. In this view, people endure hard work under substandard conditions and for subsistence wages because they have no other choice. However sympathetic this pro-immigration view may at first sound, many insist that it fails to recognize that, for most adults, the choice to immigrate is a personal one subject to more complicated factors unique to each individual.

Economic Impacts

Are immigrants, especially the low-skilled, uneducated people that are of concern to so many Americans, an economic and cultural drain on the federal government, states, and municipalities of the

United States? Or are there legitimate factors that show them to be of economic and cultural value to the nation?

President Trump and many of his supporters argue that undocumented immigrants are, indeed, bad for the American economy because they take jobs from Americans. "They're taking our jobs. They're taking our manufacturing jobs. They're taking our money. They're killing us," Trump said in 2015. However, as outlined in chapter 1, many argue that undocumented workers are in fact taking low-wage, grueling jobs that many Americans refuse to do.

Restrictionists also argue that immigrants can be a drain on the public welfare system, using tax dollars to pay for their basic needs and medical care. However, the poverty rate for immigrants in the United States was 17.3 percent in 2015, only slightly higher than the rate for the American-born population at 14.3 percent. And legally, documented immigrants must wait five years before accessing such programs as Medicaid and food stamps; undocumented immigrants are ineligible.

With regard to immigrant workers, observers of the world of business point out that there is "no finite 'lump of labor' in an economy. The presence of migrants causes new jobs to be created. Factories that may have gone abroad spring up in Arizona and Texas." Meanwhile, many employers defend the hiring of undocumented workers as a means of keeping industries afloat that might otherwise have been challenged by cheaper, imported products. They also point out that paying higher wages in order to obtain American workers would significantly raise the cost of numerous goods and services in agriculture, food processing, construction, hotels, and restaurants, among other sectors.

Some also argue that undocumented immigrants stimulate the economy in other ways. As consumers, they purchase housing, food, clothing, energy, and a wide variety of other goods and commodities, on which they pay the same taxes as any other shopper in America. Their contribution to the

Cultural Invasion or Cultural Enrichment?

The founder of the Emigration Party of Nevada, an anti-immigrant activist named Don Pauly, drives up to the Mexican consulate in Phoenix, Arizona, takes a Mexican flag out of his truck, douses it with lighter fluid, spits on it, and signals to his companion to light a match.

"We need to get rid of all those who are destroying our country," Pauly says as the red, green, and white flag of Mexico flames on the sidewalk. "We are being invaded."

Pauly, who has argued that Mexican women in the United States should be sterilized after the birth of their first child, founded just one of some 140 hate groups—white supremacists and neo-Nazis among them—that appear to have primarily racist antipathies toward Hispanic immigrants.

On a less radical level are Americans who grumble about the cultural impact of Spanish speakers on American daily life. Why, they ask, do so many public services and packaged consumer goods offer information in English and Spanish?

"When Latinos were fewer and without much money to spend, major corporations were not interested in them," writer Earl Shorris explains in *Latinos: A Biography of a People*. However, when annual spending among Hispanics jumped from $50 billion in 1980 to $800 billion in the 2000s, corporate America began to court them, and they soon entered the consumer mainstream. The decision to use Spanish to sell everything from food to entertainment then came from the purveyors of the products.

But why, vexed English speakers complain, can't Hispanics learn English? Research indicates that they do. By 2013, a record 68 percent of Hispanics in the United States spoke English proficiently, according

DEPORT AND BUILD THE WALL

Supporters of Donald Trump express their support for his proposed immigration restrictions at a rally during his 2016 run for president.

to the Pew Research Center. However, immigrant-rights advocates point out that the United States does not have an official language, so speaking English cannot be used as a means of regulating immigration or citizenship. Multilingualism and multiculturalism can actually benefit the United States, these advocates argue. Communities are culturally enriched by the presence of new foods, cuisines, ethnic music and dance, and holiday customs and celebrations.

Social Security system was estimated at $13 billion in 2010 (the most recent figured from the Social Security Administration), yet most have no hope of collecting benefits. Many also pay income taxes.

The state of North Carolina, which in 2004 had a Hispanic population of approximately six hundred thousand, about half of them undocumented, commissioned a study measuring the costs versus the contributions of its growing Hispanic population. Researchers at the University of North Carolina at Chapel Hill presented the following data. "Hispanics, legal and illegal, cost state taxpayers $817 million in 2004, with education and health care being the biggest expenses. Meanwhile, Hispanics generated $756 million in tax revenue. According to the report, that averages out to a cost to the state budget of $102 per Hispanic resident."

In fact, many argue that widespread deportation of the country's estimated 11 million undocumented immigrants could hurt the US economy. An immigration raid at Chicago's Cloverhill Bakery in June and July of 2017 forced the company to let go of eight hundred workers, about 35 percent of its workforce, because they lacked sufficient documentation. Aryzta AG, Cloverhill's parent company, reported losses exceeding $19 million as a result of this loss. "As these individuals had significant knowledge and experience of the baking process ... there has been a significant decrease in the labor efficiency and production volumes as a result of this disruption," the company reported.

By 2017, public opinion regarding immigrants had shifted, with 49 percent believing that they help the US economy and 40 percent believing that they hurt it. This marked a "near reversal," according to Gallup, of public opinion from 2005, when 49 percent of Americans believed immigrants harmed the economy while 42 percent believed that they helped.

Projections on the Future of Immigration

At the current rate of immigration, what are the projected characteristics of the population of the United States in the year 2065? The following figures are taken from a March 2016 Pew Research Center report.

In 2018, Americans were already a more ethnically and racially diverse group than ever before. Similarly, Pew reported, "The 2016 electorate will be the most diverse in U.S. history due to strong growth among Hispanic eligible voters, particularly U.S.-born youth." And diversity is expected to continue growing, with whites constituting just under 50 percent of the US population by 2055 or 2065. That means that the United States, long dominated by a white majority, will no longer have any one racial or ethnic majority.

In 2016, Hispanics constituted the largest minority in the country: 17.8 percent of the US population identified as Hispanic or Latino. However, Pew reported in 2016 that "Asians are now the only major racial or ethnic group whose numbers are rising mainly because of immigration. And while African immigrants make up a small share of the U.S. immigrant population, their numbers are also growing steadily—roughly doubling every decade since 1970." As a result, the distribution of immigrant groups is expected to change significantly. By 2055, Asians are projected to become the largest immigrant group at 36 percent of all immigrants, up from 26 percent in 2015. Both black and white immigrants are expected to see only a small increase between 2015 and 2055. Hispanic immigration, however, is expected to comprise a smaller percent of total immigration—34 percent by 2055, compared to 47 percent in 2015.

As a result, millennials—people born between 1981 and 1996—are projected to be the most racially diverse generation in US history. Today, 43 percent of millennials are nonwhite.

Chain Migration and America's Future

During his first year in office, Donald Trump called for a rollback of measures known as "chain migration." This process, officially called "family reunification," allows legal US residents and green-card holders to sponsor family members, enabling them to immigrate to the United States. In 2018, CBS News reported that "Between 60 and 70 percent of all lawful permanent immigration to the United States in the past decade has family-based roots." In 2016, more than 238,000 immigrants were family-sponsored, and nearly 580,000 were immediate relatives of American citizens.

President Trump argued that such an immigration policy threatens national security. For evidence of this, he pointed to Akayed Ullah, suspected of trying to bomb a passageway in the New York City subway in December 2017. Ullah had entered the country via chain migration through a sponsorship. Trump has argued for merit-based immigration instead, with the White House's website claiming, "The large influx of predominantly low-skilled migrants has had substantial fiscal and national security consequences." Distinctions such as this are sure to define the future of American immigration policy.

From the inception of the United States, the pressure imposed by immigration has been extraordinary and persistent. Of necessity, restrictions on legal immigration have been applied. However, the reasons that motivate people to emigrate from their countries have changed dramatically over time, spurred by wars, economic troubles, discrimination in their home countries, and many other factors. These reasons will continue to change, and US immigration policy is likely to adapt along with it, always seeking to strike that difficult balance between the needs of the many and the needs of the few, between the prosperity of American citizens and the wellbeing of those who desire to become Americans.

Glossary

alien In this case, a foreigner.

amnesty The pardoning or forgiveness of a large group of individuals by a governmental or other authority.

anti-Semitic Hostile to or prejudiced against Jews.

asylum In this case, protection granted by a nation to someone who has left their native country as a refugee.

Caucasian White-skinned, usually of European origin.

criollo A person born in the Americas who has Spanish ancestry only.

discrimination The prejudicial and unjust treatment of categories of people or things, particularly on the grounds of race, sex, ethnic background, national origin, sexual orientation, or age.

dissident A person opposed to the official policy of a nation, regime, or political entity.

embargo A ban on commercial activity or trade with a particular nation.

emigration The act of leaving one's native country to settle in another.

exodus A mass departure of people.

green card A permit allowing a person from another country to work and live in the United States on a permanent basis.

gross domestic product (GDP) The total market value of all the services and goods that a country's economy produces.

immigration The act of arriving in a foreign country to live there permanently.

incarceration The confinement of a person in prison or jail.

mestizo A person in Latin America of mixed Spanish and Native American ancestry.

nativist A person who defends the interests of the native-born inhabitants of a country over those of immigrants.

quota A fixed minimum or maximum number of people, usually of a particular group, permitted to do something, such as immigrate to a country.

refugee A person who cannot return to his or her country because of "a well-founded fear of persecution for reasons of race, religion, nationality, membership in a particular social group, or political opinion," according to the United Nations.

remittances In this case, money earned by immigrants in the country where they live that is sent to family or friends in another country.

restrictionist A person or policy favoring limits and maximums placed on immigration.

shantytown An area where poor or marginalized people have collected to build makeshift dwellings.

visa An endorsement permitting its holder to enter, leave, and/or stay in a country for a specific period of time.

Further Information

Books

Markham, Lauren. *The Far Away Brothers: Two Young Migrants and the Making of an American Life.* New York: Crown Publishing Group, 2017.

Osborne, Linda Barrett. *This Land Is Our Land: The History of American Immigration.* New York: Abrams Books for Young Readers, 2016.

Schmermund, Elizabeth, ed. *Immigrant Bans. Opposing Viewpoints.* New York: Greenhaven Publishing, 2018.

Uwiringiyimana, Sandra, and Abigail Pesta. *How Dare the Sun Rise: Memoirs of a War Child.* New York: HarperCollins Publishers, 2017.

Websites

Migration Policy Institute
https://www.migrationpolicy.org

This nonpartisan think tank analyzes immigration and migration patterns on a global scale, and offers useful research on a variety of immigration-related topics.

National Immigration Law Center
http://www.nilc.org

The NILC protects and promotes the rights and opportunities of low-income immigrants and their family members, especially with regard to employment and public benefit rights.

USA.gov: Immigration and Citizenship

https://www.usa.gov/immigration-and-citizenship

This site offers useful information on how to apply for residency, citizenship, and other documentation necessary for legal entry into the United States.

Videos

Homeland: Immigration in America

http://www.pbs.org/video/homeland-immigration-america-jobs

This fifty-four-minute PBS documentary takes a look at the roles immigrants play in American society and investigates multiple sides of the immigration debate.

Immigrant Success

https://www.history.com/topics/ellis-island/videos/immigrant-success

Learn which famous Americans began their lives as immigrants to the United States.

Think Back: America's Immigration Debate

https://www.nytimes.com/video/us/100000002517565/think-back-americas-immigration-debate.html

This video looks back at the history of immigration in the United States—including the history of resistance to specific groups of people.

Organizations

American Civil Liberties Union

125 Broad Street, 18th Floor

New York, NY 10004

(212) 549-2500

http://www.aclu.org

The ACLU is one of the nation's leading advocacy groups for the rights of immigrants, refugees, and noncitizens. A key part of its mission is to challenge unconstitutional laws and practices.

American Immigrant Control Foundation

P.O. Box 525

Monterey, VA 24465

(540) 468-2022

http://www.aicfoundation.com

The AIC Foundation represents citizens concerned with both legal and illegal immigration based on this organization's view that the nation has limited capacity to absorb newcomers.

Canadian Civil Liberties Union

90 Eglinton Ave. E

Suite 900

Toronto, ON M4P 2Y3

(416) 363-0321

http://www.ccla.org

The CCLA, founded in 1964, advocates for human rights and civil liberties throughout Canada. The organization advocates for just immigrant policies for asylum-seekers, refugees, and displaced persons.

Canadian Council for Refugees

6839 Drolet #301

Montréal, Québec H2S 2T1

(514) 277-7223

Website: http://ccrweb.ca

This national nonprofit organization seeks to protect the rights of refugees and migrants, and to aid in their resettlement in Canada.

Human Rights First

75 Broad St., 31st Floor

New York, NY 10004

(212) 845-5200

http://www.humanrightsfirst.org

Human Rights First has worked since 1978 to protect and promote fundamental human rights including those of refugees and asylum-seekers in the United States and around the world.

Mexican American Legal Defense and Education Fund

634 S. Spring Street

Los Angeles, CA 90014

(213) 629-2512

http://www.maldef.org

MAL-DEF was founded in San Antonio, Texas, in 1968 to safeguard the civil rights of Hispanics and Latinos living in the United States with regard to immigration, education, employment, and political access.

Bibliography

"Age-Sex Pyramids of Top Immigrant Origin Groups in U.S., 2016." Migration Policy Institute. Accessed April 3, 2018. https://www.migrationpolicy.org/programs/data-hub/charts/age-sex-pyramids-top-immigrant-origin-groups?width=1000&height=850&iframe=true.

Aguilar, Julián. "How Donald Trump's Border Wall Fared in the $1.3 Trillion Spending Bill He Just Signed." *Texas Tribune,* March 23, 2018. https://www.texastribune.org/2018/03/23/donald-trump-border-wall-16-million-funding-restrictions-attached.

Aleaziz, Hamed. "Immigration Agents Raid 77 Northern California Workplaces; No Arrests Reported." *SFGATE*, February 2, 2018. https://www.sfgate.com/bayarea/article/ICE-workplace-sweep-hits-Northern-California-12544863.php.

Anderson, Stuart. "Trump's Assault on Legal High-Skilled Immigration." *Reason*, October 30, 2017. http://reason.com/archives/2017/10/30/trumps-assault-on-legal-high-skilled-imm.

Badillo, Herman. *One Nation, One Standard: An Ex-Liberal on How Hispanics Can Succeed.* New York: Penguin, 2006.

Benjamin, Medea, and Nicolas J. S. Davies. "The Staggering Death Toll in Iraq." Truthout, March 19, 2018. http://www.truth-out.org/opinion/item/43882-the-staggering-death-toll-in-iraq.

Benner, Katie, and Jennifer Medina. "Trump Administration Sues California Over Immigration Laws." *New York Times*, March 6,

2018. https://www.nytimes.com/2018/03/06/us/politics/justice-department-california-sanctuary-cities.html.

Blanco, Octavio. "Why Undocumented Immigrants Pay Taxes." CNN Money, April 19, 2017. http://money.cnn.com/2017/04/19/news/economy/undocumented-immigrant-taxes/index.html.

Borjas, George J. "Yes, Immigration Hurts American Workers." *POLITICO*, September/October 2016. https://www.politico.com/magazine/story/2016/09/trump-clinton-immigration-economy-unemployment-jobs-214216.

Brachear Pashman, Manya. "Son of Immigration Activist Who Sought Sanctuary in Chicago Church to Graduate High School." *Chicago Tribune,* June 14, 2017. http://www.chicagotribune.com/news/immigration/ct-saul-arellano-graduates-high-school-met-20170614-story.html.

Cheng, Amrit. "The Muslim Ban: What Just Happened?" American Civil Liberties Union, December 6, 2017. https://www.aclu.org/blog/immigrants-rights/muslim-ban-what-just-happened.

Chishti, Muzaffar, Sarah Pierce, and Jessica Bolter. "The Obama Record on Deportations: Deporter in Chief or Not?" Migration Policy Institute, January 26, 2017. https://www.migrationpolicy.org/article/obama-record-deportations-deporter-chief-or-not.

Cohn, D'Vera, and Andrea Caumont. "10 Demographic Trends that Are Shaping the U.S. and the World." Pew Research Center, March 31, 2016. http://www.pewresearch.org/fact-tank/2016/03/31/10-demographic-trends-that-are-shaping-the-u-s-and-the-world.

Conover, Ted. "The United States of Asylum." *New York Times Magazine*, September 19, 1993.

"Countries of Birth for U.S. Immigrants, 1960-Present." Migration Policy Institute. Accessed April 9, 2018. https://www.migrationpolicy.org/programs/data-hub/charts/immigrants-countries-birth-over-time?width=1000&height=850&iframe=true.

Cumoletti, Mattea, and Jeanne Batalova. "Middle Eastern and North African Immigrants in the United States." Migration Policy Institute, January 10, 2018. https://www.migrationpolicy.org/article/middle-eastern-and-north-african-immigrants-united-states.

Dahir, Abdi Latir. "Chad Is the First African Country Taken off Trump's Travel Ban List." *Quartz*, April 11, 2018. https://qz.com/1249760/chad-removed-from-trump-travel-ban-list.

Daniels, Jeff. "US Agents Arrest More Than 200 Undocumented Immigrants, Target 122 Businesses in California Sweep." CNBC, February 16, 2018. https://www.cnbc.com/2018/02/16/federal-immigration-raids-in-southern-california-target-122-businesses.html.

Daniels, Roger. *Guarding the Golden Door: American Immigration Policy and Immigrants Since 1882.* New York: Hill and Wang, 2004.

"Darweesh v. Trump: Decision and Order." American Civil Liberties Union, January 28, 2017. https://www.aclu.org/legal-document/darweesh-v-trump-decision-and-order.

Dinnerstein, Leonard, and David M. Reimers. *Ethnic Americans: A History of Immigration and Assimilation*. New York: Dodd, Mead, 1975.

Flagg, Anna. "The Myth of the Criminal Immigrant." *New York Times*, March 30, 2018. https://www.nytimes.com/interactive/2018/03/30/upshot/crime-immigration-myth.html.

"Franklin Delano Roosevelt." Holocaust Encyclopedia, United States Holocaust Memorial Museum. Accessed April 8, 2018. https://www.ushmm.org/wlc/en/article.php?ModuleId=10007411.

Gaynor, Tim. "Nativists Fan Flames of US Immigration Debate," Boston.com, December 24, 2006.

Gomez, Alan, and Sophie Kaplan. "DACA Was Supposed to End Monday. It Didn't, but Dreamers Remain Anxious." *USA Today*, March 5, 2018. https://www.usatoday.com/story/news/nation/2018/03/05/dreamers-daca-program-march-5-end/393280002.

Gonchar, Michael. "The Debate on Dreamers: A Lesson Plan for Teaching About DACA." *New York Times*, February 21, 2018. https://www.nytimes.com/2018/02/21/learning/lesson-plans/a-lesson-plan-for-teaching-about-daca-and-dreamers.html.

Goodhue, David. "Traffickers Carrying 30 Cuban Migrants Halted by the Feds off Key Largo." *Miami Herald*, March 12, 2017. http://www.miamiherald.com/news/local/immigration/article138043748.html.

Guild, Blair. "What Is 'Chain Migration'?" CBS News, January 29, 2018. https://www.cbsnews.com/news/what-is-chain-migration-definition-visa-trump-administration-family-reunification.

"Helping Dreamers Can't Get U.S. Voters over the Wall, Quinnipiac University National Poll Finds; Support for Infrastructure Almost 10-1." Quinnipiac University Poll, January 18, 2018. https://poll.qu.edu/national/release-detail?ReleaseID=2514.

Hing, Julianne. "The Truth About Immigrants and Public Benefits." *Nation*, June 29, 2017. https://www.thenation.com/article/the-truth-about-immigrants-and-public-benefits.

History.com Staff. "Japanese Internment Camps." History.com, accessed April 8, 2018. https://www.history.com/topics/world-war-ii/japanese-american-relocation.

Hoban, Brennan. "Do Immigrants 'Steal' Jobs from American Workers?" Brookings Institution, August 24, 2017. https://www.brookings.edu/blog/brookings-now/2017/08/24/do-immigrants-steal-jobs-from-american-workers.

International Organization for Migration. "Number of Returns Exceeds Number of Displaced Iraqis: UN Migration Agency." ReliefWeb, January 12, 2018. https://reliefweb.int/report/iraq/number-returns-exceeds-number-displaced-iraqis-un-migration-agency.

"Iraq 10 Years On: In Numbers." BBC News, March 20, 2013. http://www.bbc.com/news/world-middle-east-21752819.

Jacobo, Julia, and Serena Marshall. "Nearly 700 Miles of Fencing at the US-Mexico Border Already Exist." ABC News, January 26,

2017. http://abcnews.go.com/US/700-miles-fencing-us-mexico-border-exist/story?id=45045054.

"Japanese Relocation During World War II." National Archives, April 10, 2017. https://www.archives.gov/education/lessons/japanese-relocation.

Johnson, Jenna, and Abigail Hauslohner. "'I Think Islam Hates Us': A Timeline of Trump's Comments about Islam and Muslims." *Washington Post*, May 20, 2017. https://www.washingtonpost.com/news/post-politics/wp/2017/05/20/i-think-islam-hates-us-a-timeline-of-trumps-comments-about-islam-and-muslims/?utm_term=.af60aee0f293.

Jordan, Miriam. "Most Americans Want Legal Status for 'Dreamers.' These People Don't." *New York Times*, January 25, 2018. https://www.nytimes.com/2018/01/25/us/dreamers-opponents-daca-deal.html.

Kavilanz, Parija. "ICE Pledges Immigration Crackdown on Businesses. Here's What It Looks Like." CNN Money, January 15, 2018. http://money.cnn.com/2018/01/15/news/economy/ice-immigration-work-site-crackdown/index.html.

Kessler, Glenn. "The Debate over DACA: A Guide to the Numbers Used by Politicians." *Washington Post*, January 23, 2018. https://www.washingtonpost.com/news/fact-checker/wp/2018/01/23/the-debate-over-daca-a-guide-to-the-numbers-used-by-politicians/?utm_term=.31129cca7d4f.

Kitroeff, Natalie, and Geoffrey Mohan. "Wages Rise on California Farms. Americans Still Don't Want the Job." *Los Angeles Times*,

March 17, 2017. http://www.latimes.com/projects/la-fi-farms-immigration.

Korte, Gregory, Eliza Collins, and David Jackson. "Trump Clears Up His Immigration Position: A Border Wall Must Be Part of Any DACA Deal." *USA Today*, January 10, 2018. https://www.usatoday.com/story/news/politics/2018/01/10/trump-clears-up-his-immigration-position-border-wall-must-part-any-daca-deal/1021801001.

Krikorian, Mark. "Jobs American Won't Do." *National Review Online*, January 7, 2004. http://www.nationalreview.com/comment/Krikorian 200401070923.asp.

———. "New Immigration Law? Enforce Old Ones First." *NY Daily News*, May 23, 2007.

Krogstad, Jens Manual, Renee Stepler, and Mark Hugo Lopez. "English Proficiency on the Rise Among Latinos." Pew Research Center, May 12, 2015. http://www.pewhispanic.org/2015/05/12/english-proficiency-on-the-rise-among-latinos.

Lind, Dara. "Sanctuary Cities, Explained." *Vox*, March 8, 2018. https://www.vox.com/policy-and-politics/2018/3/8/17091984/sanctuary-cities-city-state-illegal-immigration-sessions.

Ludden, Jennifer. "Communities Cite Impact of Immigration Raids." NPR *Morning Edition*, April 3, 2008. http://www.npr.org/templates/story/story.php?storyId=10292673.

Mallaby, Sebastian. "Lazy Job-Stealing Immigrants." *Washington Post,* April 30, 2007.

Marshall, Christa. "Greeley Mayor Urges Changes in ICE Raids." *Denver Post*, May 18, 2007.

Martin, Patrick. "Populist Demagogy and Immigrant-Bashing in the US: The Case of Lou Dobbs." International Committee of the Fourth International, June 16, 2006, http://www.wsws.org/articles/2006/jun2006/immi-j16.shtml.

Mau, Dhani. "U.S. Garment Production Wouldn't Be a Thing Without Migrants." Fashionista, July 4, 2017. https://fashionista.com/2017/07/american-garment-factories-production-immigrant-workers.

Mills, Nicolaus, ed. *Arguing Immigration: The Debate over the Changing Face of America.* New York: Simon & Schuster, 1994.

Nicholson, Michael D., and CAP Immigration Team. "The Facts on Immigration Today: 2017 Edition." Center for American Progress, April 20, 2017. https://www.americanprogress.org/issues/immigration/reports/2017/04/20/430736/facts-immigration-today-2017-edition.

Nickelsburg, Monica. "Trump's Immigration Crackdown May Force Amazon and Microsoft to Shift Some Workers to Canada." *GeekWire*, February 1, 2017. https://www.geekwire.com/2017/trumps-immigration-crackdown-may-force-amazon-microsoft-shift-workers-canada.

"North America: Mexico." Central Intelligence Agency, World Factbook, March 23, 2018. https://www.cia.gov/library/publications/the-world-factbook/geos/mx.html.

O'Boyle, Michael. "Migrants Changing Nebraska Town," American Renaissance, February 14, 2005. http://www.amren.com/mtnews/archives/2005/02/migrants_changi.php.

Olinger, David. "Border Wars Personal Out West." *Denver Post*, January 27, 2008. https://www.denverpost.com/2008/01/26/border-wars-personal-out-west.

Parlapiano, Alicia, and Karen Yourish. "A Typical 'Dreamer' Lives in Los Angeles, Is from Mexico and Came to the U.S. at 6 Years Old." *New York Times*, January 23, 2018. https://www.nytimes.com/interactive/2017/09/05/us/politics/who-are-the-dreamers.html.

Pear, Robert, and Jim Rutenberg. "Senators in Bipartisan Deal on Immigration Bill." *New York Times,* May 18, 2007. https://www.nytimes.com/2007/05/18/washington/18immig.html.

Perl, Lila. *Behind Barbed Wire: The Story of Japanese-American Internment During World War II.* Tarrytown, NY: Marshall Cavendish, 2003.

———. *North Across the Border: The Story of the Mexican Americans.* Tarrytown, NY: Marshall Cavendish, 2002.

———. *To the Golden Mountain: The Story of the Chinese Who Built the Transcontinental Railroad.* Tarrytown, NY: Marshall Cavendish, 2003.

"Photos: 68 People Arrested at DACA Protest in Washington, D.C." *Arizona Daily Star,* March 6, 2018. http://tucson.com/news/government-and-politics/photos-people-arrested-at-daca-protest-in-washington-d-c/collection_245cdb66-2164-11e8-bca1-87a8d6f6db72.html#1.

"Place of Birth for Foreign-Born Population in the United States: Universe—Foreign-born population excluding population born at sea." United States Census Bureau, 2016 American Community Survey 1-Year Estimates, 2016. https://factfinder. census.gov/faces/tableservices/jsf/pages/productview. xhtml?pid=ACS_15_1YR_B05006&prodType=table.

Posey, Erica. "Oral Argument on the Muslim Ban: What You Need to Know." Brennan Center for Justice, May 8, 2017. https://www. brennancenter.org/blog/oral-argument-muslim-ban-what-you-need-know.

"Quick Facts: United States." United States Census Bureau, July 1, 2016. https://www.census.gov/quickfacts/fact/table/US /PST045216#qf-headnote-b.

Quinones, Sam. *Antonio's Gun and Delfino's Dream: True Tales of Mexican Immigration.* Albuquerque: University of New Mexico Press, 2007.

Radford, Jynnah, and Jens Manuel Krogstad. "Afghans Who Worked for U.S. Government Make up Growing Share of Special Immigrant Visa Recipients." Pew Research Center, December 11, 2017. http://www.pewresearch.org/fact-tank/2017/12/11/ afghans-who-worked-for-u-s-government-make-up-growing-share-of-special-immigrant-visa-recipients.

Ramos, Jorge. *The Other Face of America: Chronicles of the Immigrants Shaping Our Future.* New York: HarperCollins, 2002.

"Remarks by the President on Immigration." White House Office of the Press Secretary, June 15, 2012. https://obamawhitehouse. archives.gov/the-press-office/2012/06/15/remarks-president-immigration.

"Report: Remittances to Latin America and the Caribbean in 2017." *Dialogue*, January 24, 2018. https://www.thedialogue.org/resources/remittances-to-latin-america-and-the-caribbean-in-2017.

Reuters. "Trump Defends Immigration Ban as 'Not About Religion.'" *Newsweek*, January 29, 2017. http://www.newsweek.com/trump-defends-immigration-ban-not-religion-549875.

Rivera, Geraldo. *His Panic: Why Americans Fear Hispanics in the US.* New York: Celebra, Penguin, 2008.

Rives, Karin. "Part 1: Jobs Lure Illegal Immigrants to State." *News & Observer*, March 6, 2006. http://www.unc.edu/world/N&O%20 Hispanics%20series.pdf.

Roberts, Sam. *Who We Are Now: The Changing Face of America in the 21st Century.* New York: Holt, 2004.

Rodriguez, Gregory. *Mongrels, Bastards, Orphans, and Vagabonds: Mexican Immigration and the Future of Race in America.* New York: Pantheon, 2007.

Schulz, Jennifer, and Jeanne Batalova. "Haitian Immigrants in the United States." Migration Policy Institute, August 2, 2017. https://www.migrationpolicy.org/article/haitian-immigrants-united-states.

Shorris, Earl. *Latinos: A Biography of a People.* New York: W. W. Norton, 1992.

Smith, Robert Courtney. *Mexican New York: Transnational Lives of New Immigrants.* Berkeley, CA: University of California Press, 2006.

Stephen, Lynn. "The Gaze of Surveillance in the Lives of Mexican Immigrant Workers." Society for International Development, 2004. http://www.sidint.org/development.

"Swift Responds to Plant Raids." (Greeley, CO) Tribune, December 12, 2006. https://www.greeleytribune.com/news/local/swift-responds-to-plant-raids.

Talbot, Margaret. "The Lost Children." New Yorker, March 3, 2008. https://www.newyorker.com/magazine/2008/03/03/the-lost-children.

Thompson, Gabriel. There's No José Here: Following the Hidden Lives of Mexican Immigrants. New York: Nation Books, 2007.

Truman, Harry S. "Statement by the President Upon Signing the Displaced Persons Act, June 25, 1948." American Presidency Project. Accessed January 24, 2008. http://www.presidency.ucsb.edu/ws/?pid=12942.

Valverde, Miriam. "Sen. Tom Cotton Misleads in Claim about Dream Act Amnesty." *PolitiFact*, September 26, 2017. http://www.politifact.com/truth-o-meter/statements/2017/sep/26/tom-cotton/sen-tom-cotton-misleads-claim-about-dream-act-amne.

"Vigilantes Gather in Arizona." Anti-Defamation League, April 7, 2005. http://www.adl.org/learn/extremism_in_the_news/ White_Supremacy/arizona_vigilantes_40705.htm?LEARN_ Cat=Extremism&LEARN_SubCat=Extremism_in_the_News.

Wolf, Richard. "Battle over Trump's Immigration Travel Ban Escalates." *USA Today*, September 11, 2017. https://www. usatoday.com/story/news/politics/2017/09/11/battle-over- trumps-immigration-travel-ban-escalates/655254001.

Zong, Jie, Jeanne Batalova, and Jeffrey Hallock. "Frequently Requested Statistics on Immigrants and Immigration in the United States." Migration Policy Institute, February 8, 2018. https://www .migrationpolicy.org/article/frequently-requested-statistics -immigrants-and-immigration-united-states#Demographic.

Index

Page numbers in **boldface** are illustrations

About the Authors

Lila Perl published more than sixty books for young people and adults, including fiction and nonfiction. Her nonfiction writings were mainly in the fields of social history, family memoir, and biography. Two of her books have been honored with American Library Association Notable awards. Ten titles have been selected as Notable Children's Trade Books in the Field of Social Studies. Lila Perl has also received a Boston Globe Horn Book award, a Sidney Taylor Committee award, and a Young Adults' Choice award from the International Reading Association. The New York Public Library has cited her work among Best Books for the Teen Age.

Erin L. McCoy is a literature, language, and cultural studies educator and an award-winning photojournalist and poet. She holds a master of arts degree in Hispanic studies and a master of fine arts degree in creative writing from the University of Washington. She has edited nearly twenty nonfiction books for young adults, including *The Mexican-American War and The Israel-Palestine Border Conflict* from the Redrawing the Map series with Cavendish Square Publishing. She is from Louisville, Kentucky.